THE TRUTH IS

1. Leveling up your craft to write a story that lives long after you've left the planet is what some might call a ridiculous goal.

2. You will not tell that story after reading just one how-to-write book.

3. You will not tell that story as the result of taking one seminar.

4. You know creating a timeless work of art will require the dedication of a world-class athlete. You will be training your mind with as much ferocity and single-minded purpose as an Olympic gold medal hopeful. That kind of cognitive regimen excites you, but you just haven't found a convincing storytelling dojo to do that work.

5. The path to leveling up your creative craft is a dark and treacherous one. You've been at it a long time, and it often feels like you're wearing three-dimensional horse blinders. More times than you'd like to admit, you're not sure if you're moving north or south or east or west. And the worst part? You can't see anyone else, anywhere, going through what you're going through. You're all alone.

WELCOME TO THE STORY GRID UNIVERSE
HERE'S HOW WE CONTEND WITH THOSE TRUTHS

1. We believe we find meaning in the pursuit of creations that last longer than we do. This is *not* ridiculous. Seizing opportunities and overcoming obstacles as we stretch ourselves to reach for seemingly unreachable creations is transformational. We believe this pursuit is the most valuable and honorable way to spend our time here. Even if—especially if—we never reach our lofty creative goals.

2. Writing just one story isn't going to take us to the top. We're moving from point A to Point A^{5000}. We've got lots of mountains to climb, lots of rivers and oceans to cross, and many deep dark forests to traverse along the way. We need topographic guides, and if they're not available, we'll have to figure out how to write them ourselves.

3. We're drawn to seminars to consume the imparted wisdom of an icon in the arena, but we leave with something far more valuable than the curriculum. We get to meet the universe's other pilgrims and compare notes on the terrain.

4. The Story Grid Universe has a virtual dojo, a university in which to work out and get stronger—a place to stumble, correct mistakes, and stumble

again, until the moves become automatic and mesmerizing to outside observers.

5. The Story Grid Universe has a performance space, a publishing house dedicated to leveling up the craft with clear boundaries of progress and the ancillary reference resources to pack for each project mission. There are an infinite number of paths to where you want to be, with a story that works. Seeing how others have made it down their own yellow-brick roads to release their creations into the timeless creative cosmos will help keep you on the straight and narrow path.

All are welcome—the more, the merrier. But please abide by the golden rule:
Put the work above all else, and trust the process.

HARRY POTTER AND THE SORCERER'S STONE

A STORY GRID MASTERWORK ANALYSIS GUIDE

SAVANNAH GILBO

Edited by
ABIGAIL K. PERRY

STORY GRID

Story Grid Publishing LLC
Nashville, TN

Copyright (c) 2024 Story Grid Publishing
Cover Design by Timothy Hsu
Edited by Abigail K. Perry

All Rights Reserved

First Story Grid Publishing Paperback Edition
July 2024

For Information About Special Discount for Bulk Purchases,

Please visit www.storygridpublishing.com

Paperback ISBN: 978-1-64501-098-2
Ebook ISBN: 978-1-64501-099-9

For

All Past, Present, and Future Story Nerds

HOW TO READ THIS GUIDE

There are two ways to read this book.

First, enjoy the novel without worrying about any of the Story Grid stuff.

Second, read each scene thinking about the Story Grid principles.

The bolded words in each scene correspond to a particular element that we include in the Story Grid Spreadsheet. To see the entire Story Grid Spreadsheet for *Harry Potter and the Sorcerer's Stone*, as well as the Story Grid Foolscap and Infographic, visit https://www.storygrid.com/master work/harry-potter-and-the-sorcerers-stone/. These resources are far too long and detailed to include in this book, but they are important tools we use to analyze the story.

At the conclusion of each scene, we've included an additional section entitled *Analyzing the Scene*. In our Story Event and Five Commandments analysis, we walk you through critical information to help you understand the decisions J.K. Rowling made, scene by scene, to construct *Harry Potter and the Sorcerer's Stone* and generate excitement, intrigue, and catharsis to satisfy readers for decades.

Before reading our analysis, we highly recommend reading *Harry Potter and the Sorcerer's Stone* and using the Story Grid Scene Analysis Worksheet PDF to analyze each scene. You can download that worksheet here: https://www.storygrid.com/masterwork/scene-analysis-worksheet/.

One of the best ways to learn new skills is through deliberate practice. When you read a scene, take your best shot at identifying its Story Event and Five Commandments, and *then* read our analysis, it creates a short feedback loop that helps you get better at analyzing scenes. As you gain a deeper understanding of how scenes work and apply it to your daily writing practice, the scenes you write will get better.

For those unfamiliar with Story Grid's four Story Event questions and Five Commandments of Storytelling, you can read about them in the book *Story Grid 101* (a free download on the Story Grid site), in *The Story Grid: What Good Editors Know*, or in articles on the site (https://www.storygrid.com/).

INTRODUCTION

Readers all around the world first discovered the magic of J.K. Rowling's Harry Potter series with the UK release of *Harry Potter and the Philosopher's Stone* in 1997. Since then, the Harry Potter series has reached monumental heights that were never before considered possible—especially for a middle-grade fantasy novel.

According to a 2018 article on the Wizarding World website, more than five hundred million Harry Potter books have been sold worldwide (180 million in the US alone) and the series has been translated into more than eighty languages. The seven books (not counting special editions and boxed sets) have spent a combined 1,739 weeks on *USA Today's* Best-Selling Books list, with *Harry Potter and the Sorcerer's Stone* (the US edition of book one) logging the most at 481 weeks. The series has also given rise to eight movies, one spin off movie series (*Fantastic Beasts and Where to Find Them*), a Broadway show (*Harry Potter and the Cursed Child*), as well as branded theme parks all around the world.

So, why was this first book—and later the series—such a hit? Why does it *still* resonate with us almost thirty years later? And more importantly, what can we writers learn from a story like this?

Harry Potter and the Sorcerer's Stone is what we in the Story Grid Universe call a Masterwork—a story that "works" and transcends the time and culture of its author. In this analysis guide, we're going to dive deep into the pages of this best-selling novel to discover how and (more importantly) why it works. To do this, we'll study it from both the macro and micro perspective through the lens of the Action genre. We'll see how this story fits within the Action genre framework, break it down on a scene-by-scene basis, and identify all the obligatory moments and conventions within the story that work together to create the whole.

We'll explore how Rowling developed a cast of quirky characters with varied backgrounds, ages, professions, emotions, and viewpoints, which helps readers of all ages and cultures relate. We'll look at how she crafted the perfect setting ripe for conflict and life-and-death stakes as well as how she immersed readers in that setting without overwhelming them or info dumping. We'll even explore how no detail, no matter how big or small, in Rowling's world is wasted.

But don't worry. If you're not writing fantasy, an Action story, or a book meant for middle-grade readers, you will still find a ton of value in this analysis guide. Most of the principles and techniques we'll go over can apply to writers and stories across all age ranges and genres of commercial fiction. So, let's dive in, starting with what makes *Harry Potter and the Sorcerer's Stone* an Action story Masterwork.

WHAT MAKES HARRY POTTER AND THE SORCERER'S STONE AN ACTION STORY MASTERWORK?

Harry Potter and the Sorcerer's Stone is a story about what it takes to survive—and how to become the best version of yourself in that fight for survival. From the very first page, readers learn that a very powerful wizard named Lord Voldemort murdered both of Harry's parents, and tried but failed to kill him, too. Even though the wizarding world is celebrating, it's clear Voldemort is still out there, waiting for another opportunity to return to power.

We pick up Harry's story eleven years later, when he gets a letter inviting him back into the wizarding world to study magic at Hogwarts School of Witchcraft and Wizardry. Once there, he must literally (and figuratively) figure out how to survive (core need) all the challenges that come his way—no matter how big or small.

Learning how to wield magic while being around other students who can also use magic automatically raises the risk of injury or harm. There are also dangerous places like the Forbidden Forest and the "off-limits" third-floor corridor—not to mention fantastic beasts like unicorns, trolls, and dragons that pose potential threats for Harry and his friends, too.

But the biggest conflict Harry faces throughout the story is personal.

Draco Malfoy and his gang of bullies pick on Harry from day one, putting his safety and his place at Hogwarts at risk. Professor Snape seems determined to make Harry's life miserable and becomes the number one suspect when Harry realizes the Sorcerer's Stone is at Hogwarts and is in jeopardy of being stolen. When the threat on the Sorcerer's Stone escalates, Harry must face the biggest challenge of all, Lord Voldemort, to keep his new friends and himself safe.

In every scene, Harry and his friends must act in response to unexpected events, and their choices make their survival more or less likely. This generates excitement in readers (core emotion)—especially in the story's global climax when Harry outwits and defeats Voldemort, saving the Sorcerer's Stone (core event).

But all of that being said, this story isn't just about how Harry manages to survive a life-threatening encounter with Lord Voldemort. Nor is it just about how he navigates dangerous magical beasts or bullies who want to ruin his life—whether they're eleven-year-old students or professors who harbor misplaced grudges.

It's also about accepting yourself and having the courage to take action even when you're unsure and faced with seemingly impossible conflict. It's about what it means to let go of a life that could have been—and accepting what *is*. Dumbledore aptly summarizes this lesson for us in chapter twelve, "The Mirror of Erised," when he says, "It does not do to dwell on dreams and forget to live, remember that." Simply put, Harry cannot keep wishing for the life he's always wanted (two loving parents and no scar on his forehead). He has to learn to deal with and accept the hand he's been dealt—fame and reputation included.

That means an internal Worldview arc is present in this story, too. Rowling masterfully intertwines Harry's inner growth with his ability to solve the external conflict (preventing Voldemort from stealing the stone)—and *this* makes the story impactful.

In the beginning of the story, Harry doesn't believe he's capable of living up to his reputation as The Boy Who Lived. He doesn't remember the night Voldemort killed his parents, and he has no idea what he did to cause Voldemort's downfall. But the entire wizarding world thinks he's a hero—something that Harry just can't reconcile. Because of this, he relies on the adults in his life to solve problems and do the right thing to ensure his (and everyone else's) survival, even when he has important information they don't have.

But when Dumbledore leaves the castle (in chapter sixteen "Through the Trapdoor"), Harry must band together with his friends, Ron and Hermione, to keep the Sorcerer's Stone safe. Together, they demonstrate a great deal of courage, creativity, and out-of-the-box thinking when they sneak past Fluffy, fight their way out of Devil's Snare, catch a specific flying key among hundreds, win a life-sized (and life-threatening) game of wizard's chess, and choose the correct potion—all so that they can prevent Voldemort from getting the Sorcerer's Stone.

Once Harry goes alone into the final chamber, he has no choice but to step into his role as The Boy Who Lived, and he must use everything he's got to outwit and defeat Voldemort. If Harry hadn't learned to accept his past (the loss of his parents) and learned to own his identity (The Boy Who Lived), he wouldn't have been able to save the stone by looking in the mirror and seeing it appear in his pocket. Instead, he would have seen his deceased family like he did in chapter twelve, "The Mirror of Erised." Not only does this show us Harry's growth from page one, but it also shows us he's willing to sacrifice something important to him to help his friends and the greater wizarding world survive. This makes Harry the perfect Action story hero.

So, although this story presents us with a lot of excitement, action, and wonder, it's also a story about how the external events of the plot help Harry grow and change—and how that growth allows him to step into who he was meant to be. This is where the real magic happens. It's a recipe for what it takes to survive, *and* it shows us how a poor orphaned boy can make heroic choices in the face of great adversity and evil.

Even though readers themselves aren't up against powerful dark wizards, this story is still incredibly relevant today. We've all had moments of self-doubt, longing, and fear, even if we haven't stood between the most powerful Dark Lord and the immortality-giving Sorcerer's Stone. We all want the recipe for what it takes to survive, but more than that, we want to thrive. And that's exactly what *Harry Potter and the Sorcerer's Stone* shows us how to do.

So, with all of that in mind, let's talk about how to *write* an Action story that works. And to do that, we're going to take a look at the Action story Framework.

THE ACTION STORY FRAMEWORK

Action stories are all about survival. They center around a protagonist who faces life-or-death stakes and who must sacrifice to survive. The underlying question in every Action story is something like: How does a person overcome the powerful external forces intent on killing them and other innocent victims? What does it take for that person to survive and thrive?

As laid out in the ACTION BEAT, we know that:

- The **CORE NEED** of an Action story is survival. The protagonist both wants and needs to defeat the antagonist to save themselves and others as well as to restore their individual and/or collective agency. To do so, they'll have to find the courage to realize and activate their inner potential.

- The **CORE VALUE** of an Action story is death to life. The spectrum of values in between life and death includes things like the risk of injury, illness, and unconsciousness. Damnation, or a fate worse than death, isn't usually at play in this genre, but readers should understand what a fate worse than death would mean for the protagonist, even if we never see that fate as an option on the page.

- The **CORE EMOTION** of an Action story is excitement. This is the main feeling readers want to experience while reading an Action story—especially in the set-piece action sequences and in the big climactic moment (core event) at the end of the story.

- The **CORE EVENT** of an Action story is a scene in which the protagonist (hero) is at the mercy of the antagonist (villain)—and the protagonist either survives or dies trying. This moment forces the protagonist to choose whether to express their special gift, usually by sacrificing something, which is usually their inner obstacle, to defeat the antagonist.

- The **CONTROLLING IDEA (or THEME)** of an Action story is a one-sentence summary of how and why the protagonist survives (or not). For example, "Life is preserved when the protagonist makes a sacrifice to overpower or outwit their external and internal antagonists." Or, "Death results when the protagonist lacks the courage to sacrifice for the survival of self and others."

Now, once you have your global genre in mind, you can use the framework it gives you to see how your story should start (a force of antagonism provides a threat to the protagonist's life) and even how it ends because you already know the core event (the hero at the mercy of the villain). Your controlling idea gives you insight into how and why the change throughout your story will occur as well as what kind of lesson or message readers will walk away with (a.k.a. your theme). But these external and internal changes your protagonist experiences won't happen for no reason—or without some preexisting conditions that we call genre conventions—so let's take a look at those next.

ACTION STORY CONVENTIONS

Genre conventions are the settings, character roles, and circumstances that help you express your story's controlling idea (or theme) by creating the potential for a specific kind of change throughout your story. In The Story Grid universe, we talk about "selective constraints" that help us define the central conflict in a story and put the protagonist's core need at stake as well as "enabling constraints" that help the protagonist solve their problems (and survive). In an Action story, you need to include these conventions:

- A physical and social environment that puts the protagonist's core need (survival) at stake
- Dueling hierarchies (power versus growth) that help highlight opportunities for conflict
- Multidimensional characters who are in conflict with each other
- Plot events and circumstances that force their (external and internal) conflict to the surface

Essentially, these conventions tell us an Action story can't exist in a harmonious world. Instead, there should be a bubbling sense among the characters on the page (and within the reader's mind) that something negative is about to happen—that conflicting goals, values, and worldviews are about to clash. And this clashing will require both the protagonist and antagonist to apply their opposing agency while possibly even overcoming any internal obstacles that are holding them back in order to succeed. But in most cases, only one of them can. So, with that in mind, let's take a look at how these conventions show up in *Harry Potter and the Sorcerer's Stone*.

WORLD-BUILDING: HOW ROWLING BUILT A WORLD RIPE FOR LIFE-OR-DEATH CONFLICTS

Harry Potter and the Sorcerer's Stone was not the first middle-grade novel to feature a battle between good and evil, or even a magical boarding school, but much of what we imagine when we think of witches and wizards or fantastic beasts is the result of the world Rowling created. In fact, many readers cite Rowling's world-building as the lure that initially drew them into the *Harry Potter* series—and rightly so. Each book is filled with such wonderful details that it's easy for readers to feel fully immersed in Harry's world and believe they're truly living among witches and wizards, giants and ghosts, and dragons and unicorns.

But there's more to this story world than just magic and fantastic beasts. The setting Rowling created is full of opportunities that create life-or-death problems for Harry and his friends to face as well.

Most of the story takes place at Hogwarts—a school where young witches and wizards learn to use magic and can harm each other with magic, whether accidentally or on purpose. Fantastic beasts on the school grounds can injure the students if they're not careful, and a handful of "off-limits" settings like the third-floor-corridor and the Forbidden Forest are ripe with the potential for danger. They also have a full-contact sport called Quidditch that students play while flying high up in the air on broomsticks with little to no safety measures in place. And that's just the physical environment.

Within the school system, the teachers are in charge, and the students don't have as much agency as the adults do. This kind of setting (and power divide) makes it difficult for young people to learn how to trust themselves as well as think and act for themselves. In Harry's case, he relies on the adults in his life for most decisions, even when he has more information than they do. This creates inner conflict for Harry. He has information and ideas that could help him and his friends survive, but his default response is to rely on the adults as authority figures to decide what's important or when to take action.

At first, this makes it hard for Harry to self-actualize and fulfill his potential as an individual. But as the story continues, the need to survive forces Harry to start trusting his intuition and start taking actions for the good of himself and his friends. In other words, it requires him to start taking back some of his agency and start making decisions—and facing the consequences of those decisions—without looking to the adults for solutions. And the more he does this, or the more he acts on his own instincts and ideas, the more confidence and skill he gains, which will eventually help him face and defeat Voldemort.

Now, all of that being said, what about everything else?

If you've read any of the Harry Potter books, it's obvious that Rowling put an incredible amount of thought behind each of the elements in her story world, but this doesn't mean she had *everything* figured out while writing book one. If you want to build a story world like Rowling, my best advice is to focus on the elements that are relevant to your plot, characters, and theme. Then spread out from there as needed.

For example, in *Harry Potter and the Sorcerer's Stone*, we learn of the Ministry of Magic, but Rowling doesn't tell us about all the different jobs people perform there, that each floor corresponds to a different department, or that one of the ways you enter the Ministry is by flushing yourself down the toilet. Readers don't need to know any of this yet because it's not relevant to what happens in this first book.

However, readers *do* learn all about the Hogwarts Houses, the different ghosts that haunt the halls, the layout of the school grounds (specifically about a Forbidden Forest and a third-floor corridor that are off limits to students), and about a sport called Quidditch. She went deep into the development of these world-building elements versus others because they're relevant to (and affect) the characters, plot, and theme of this first book.

The other thing we can learn from Rowling is that few of her world-building details are "just for fun." In fact, most of her world-building details serve more than one purpose. For example, in chapter six, "The Journey from Platform Nine and Three-Quarters," Harry doesn't just buy a bar of chocolate from the snack cart. He buys a Chocolate Frog card that hides the name of a person (Nicolas Flamel), which is a major plot clue.

In chapter twelve, "The Mirror of Erised," Harry doesn't learn to play just any old board game. He learns to play wizard's chess that will later be one of the obstacles he has to pass through to get to the final chamber in the global climax. Nothing in this story is random, and thus, everything about Harry's world feels cohesive from the reader's perspective.

Like Rowling, we too can create an enchanting world that draws readers into our story. But to do that, we need to spend time fleshing out the parts of our world that affect the global story—our characters, plot, and theme—rather than bogging them down with too much information. We also need to be mindful of our target audience and their learning curve when we introduce them to our characters and story world. A "learning curve" describes how long it takes a reader to get up to speed on the nuances of a story world—and for middle-grade readers, it's very shallow. This means that if you're writing for middle-grade readers, you'll want to introduce your story world a bit slower than you would if you were writing for adults or young adults. We'll talk about this more later in the scene-by-scene analysis.

So, yes, Rowling is a master of building fantastic story worlds. But a fantastic world of magical spells and made-up creatures means nothing without compelling characters to pull readers into it. Let's talk about that next.

CHARACTER DEVELOPMENT: HOW ROWLING CREATED A CAST OF COMPELLING CHARACTERS

We can't talk about *Harry Potter and the Sorcerer's Stone* (or any book, really) without talking about its characters. Specifically, we need to look at how Rowling developed the Action genre's three primary roles—the hero, victim, and villain—and how those three roles work together to create the push-pull, cause-and-effect dynamic that fuels the entire story.

1 - Harry Potter as the Hero

In an Action story, the protagonist (or hero) is someone who both wants and needs to defeat the antagonist to save themselves and others. To do so, they'll have to find the courage to realize and activate their inner potential, likely sacrificing something in the process. In an Action story with an internal arc, the protagonist will need to overcome (or sacrifice) their inner obstacle, or the lie, misbelief or outdated worldview that's keeping them from realizing their potential.

Harry Potter is the perfect example of a middle-grade Action story hero with an internal arc because he does exactly that. He's an underdog character who has to overcome (or sacrifice) his inner obstacle, step into his role as The Boy Who Lived, and go head-to-head with Voldemort to prevent him from getting the Sorcerer's Stone. In the process, he'll save his own life and the wizarding world.

In the beginning of the story, Harry seems to be a very unlikely hero. He's an unloved and unwanted eleven-year-old boy living in the cupboard underneath the stairs at his aunt and uncle's house. He has no idea that he's special or destined for great things. In fact, everything that makes him special makes him feel weird and different, and we all know the Dursleys don't tolerate or abide by anything weird or different.

However, once Harry gets his Hogwarts acceptance letter and learns the truth about his past, everything starts to change. Harry views the opportunity to go to Hogwarts as a way to finally get what he wants—a place to belong and maybe even some friends. But with this opportunity comes fame and a reputation Harry can't quite internalize or reconcile. Somehow, he's responsible for the downfall of a very powerful dark wizard named Voldemort, yet he can't even remember the night when everything happened. This inability to reconcile his reputation with who he believes himself to be gives rise to Harry's inner obstacle that will be the primary source of inner conflict Harry faces throughout the story.

Once Harry gets to Hogwarts, he faces a whole lot of external conflict that puts pressure on his internal obstacle. He has no idea how the wizarding world works, one of his professors seems to hate him (Snape), and he's constantly bullied by another first-year student (Draco Malfoy). However, just like in real life, when characters face and overcome conflict, they grow. This is the crux of character development. Character development occurs when your character, through the external plot events of your story, makes choices—right or wrong—and ends up changing because of their experience.

So, because of the conflict Harry faces, he grows in both confidence and skill so that, in the end, he's prepared to face Voldemort. When he does, Harry's loyal friends are right there by his side, aiding his survival. Having friendships and the ability to love is Harry's true nature—and what distinguishes him from Voldemort. Harry loves and is loved by many. He saves lives while Voldemort destroys them.

When crafting your own Action story protagonist, it's helpful to consider what they want, what they value, and what they're willing to do (and are capable of doing) in the face of danger. It's also helpful to think about the similarities and differences between your protagonist and antagonist because this is where you can highlight opposite sides of your story's theme, find areas of conflicting goals and/or values, and so much more.

2 - Voldemort as the Villain

In an Action story, the antagonist (or villain) is someone who's willing to deprive others of their agency—through force, coercion, or charismatic persuasion—to get what they want.

Voldemort is the primary antagonist (villain) and source of conflict Harry faces in *Harry Potter and the Sorcerer's Stone*. He's willing to do whatever it takes to get his hands on the Sorcerer's Stone—even if that means depriving others of their agency or life. However, because of the events that happened before page one, Voldemort is too weak to apply the constant, never-ceasing, daily pressure needed to force Harry to grow and change. This is where Draco Malfoy and Severus Snape come in.

Both Snape and Draco are there, each and every day, to create chaos, torment Harry, and challenge him to grow and change. Snape forces Harry to learn skills that he otherwise would not, to open his mind to another way of being, and to release his judgments of people based on their appearance or Hogwarts house. If not for Snape's daily pressure within the halls of Hogwarts, Harry would face almost no adult opposition. Thus, Snape is the adult counterpoint to Draco's more youthful bullying, and both help Harry take one step forward in his character arc in this first book.

Operating in the background of all of this is Professor Quirrell, who serves under Voldemort, and who is the main shapeshifter in this book. Quirrell's ability to disarm people with his friendly and meek manner makes him especially dangerous. He can literally hide in plain sight and pursue the Sorcerer's Stone for Voldemort without raising too much suspicion. Not only that, but using Quirrell as a surrogate body for Voldemort (and stripping Voldemort of all of his power) allowed Rowling to get away with an eleven-year-old boy plausibly defeating this immensely powerful and dark wizard (Voldemort). Throughout the series, as Harry grows in his knowledge and magical skills, so too does Voldemort transform from parasite to something more. Thus, Harry does not have to face a fully powerful Dark Lord until he's much more skilled and powerful himself. This is something to keep in mind if you're writing a series that features a powerful antagonist and a young or inexperienced protagonist.

3 - Harry (and the wizarding world) as the Victim

In an Action story, "the victim" is any character or group of characters who have lost their ability to solve problems, meet their needs, and adapt to a changing environment.

In *Harry Potter and the Sorcerer's Stone*, the stakes are both personal and global. If Harry does not embrace his identity and defeat Voldemort, he will surely die. But it's a little bit hard for Harry to act when he's just a student who doesn't have that much agency to begin with. In fact, every time he brings one of his concerns to a teacher, he's dismissed and told not to worry about it. Because of this, Harry's attempts to achieve his goal of preventing Voldemort from getting the stone are made that much harder because his own agency is restricted.

But Rowling took this one step further and gave Harry a community of people who will also benefit from Voldemort's downfall. In fact, she filled her world with *hundreds* of characters—novice witches and wizards who are aching to learn the ins and outs of magic, a half-giant gamekeeper who is a little bit too obsessed with magical creatures, dragons who breathe fire, and a greasy-haired professor who picks on Harry like it's his day job.

There's literally a character for every kind of reader to relate to, no matter their age or culture—and this is part of what makes the *Harry Potter* series so relatable. For example, Hermione is logical, smart, and bookish while Ron is more chaotic and struggles to keep up with his course work. Hagrid has a penchant for breaking rules while someone like Filch or McGonagall love following them. Professor Quirrell has a shy, nervous demeanor while someone like Professor Snape is more serious and bold.

Rowling fleshed out her supporting cast of characters with great care and detail. Each character has their own fully realized backstory along with clear goals, motivation, and conflict that makes them feel real. For example, Hermione, the only witch in her family, is thrust into an unfamiliar world where she is left out and unpopular. Knowledge is her only power, so she initially seeks to possess it above all else. Throughout the story, she learns that friendship and bravery trump books and cleverness, and she uses this hard-earned knowledge to help others who are left-out and powerless.

That being said, a high character count is *not* the secret to a well-crafted story. Instead, the breadth of fully fleshed out characters helps readers understand the stakes. Both Wizards and Muggles alike will enjoy a more peaceful world when Voldemort is no longer a threat.

This type of character work takes time, for sure. For Rowling, there were six years between the moment she first "met" Harry on that famous train ride from Manchester to London to the time *Harry Potter and the Philosopher's Stone* was published in the UK. That means she had *years* to get fully acquainted with Harry and his friends—to develop their similarities and differences and to plot their interactions. But the good news is that it doesn't have to take you years and years to do this kind of character work. If you can drill down into these three key roles—hero, victim, and villain— as well their relationships with other characters, you'll be in a much better position to craft a story that works.

Also, keep in mind that although you must have these three key roles, different characters can play these roles from scene to scene. This helps add dimension and nuance to your story. For example, there are times that Hermione and Neville play the role of the antagonist within a scene. They aren't "bad" characters, they're just simply in the way of Harry getting what he wants in that particular scene.

So, the key takeaway here is that if your characters fall flat, no matter how exciting your plot or how fast your pacing, a reader will put the story down and likely never pick it up again. So, like Rowling, we should aim to create compelling, three-dimensional characters that readers can relate to and invest their time in. We may not have a cast of hundreds, but we *can* infuse each of our characters with realistic goals, motivations, and emotional depth to make them impactful.

PLOT CATALYSTS

Now let's examine the plot catalysts that make things even harder for the protagonist. Plot catalysts are things that naturally arise from the environment to create conflict and force the protagonist to switch up their tactics in order to reach their goals. In other words, they put pressure on the protagonist to grow, change, and start making *different* choices as well as taking different actions that "show" readers how they've grown and changed.

When writing an Action story, you'll need to include three main plot catalysts: a speech in praise of the villain, a ticking clock or deadline, and one or more set-piece action sequences. Let's take a look at how these plot catalysts show up in *Harry Potter and the Sorcerer's Stone*.

1 - The Speech in Praise of the Villain

In an Action story, the speech in praise of the villain helps to define the large power divide between the protagonist and the antagonist. It puts pressure on and motivates the protagonist to level up their knowledge and skills before facing the antagonist. In many cases, we learn what the antagonist wants (and why they want it) during the speech in praise of the villain, but not always.

In chapter four, "The Keeper of the Keys," Hagrid says, "There was this wizard who went... bad. As bad as you could go. Worse. Worse than worse."

His name was Voldemort, and about twenty years ago, he "started lookin' fer followers. Got 'em, too—some were afraid, some just wanted a bit o' his power, 'cause he was getting himself power, all right. Dark days, Harry. Didn't know who ter trust, didn't dare get friendly with strange wizards or witches... terrible things happened. He was takin' over. Course, some stood up to him—an' he killed 'em. Horribly. One o' the only safe places left was Hogwarts. Reckon Dumbledore's the only one You-Know-Who was afraid of. Didn't dare try takin' the school, not jus' then, anyway." And then he goes on to tell Harry about how Voldemort killed Harry's parents, and how "no one ever lived after he decided ter kill 'em, no one except you, an' he killed some o' the best witches an' wizards of the age..."

This "speech" shows us that Voldemort is a *very* powerful wizard. And later, when we learn that Voldemort wants the Sorcerer's Stone so he can come back to life and power, it helps us understand what's at stake. If Voldemort succeeds, terrible things will happen, and life as Harry (and the wizarding world) knows it will essentially be over.

2 - A Deadline or Ticking Clock

In an Action story, a deadline or a ticking clock helps add tension to the plot by giving the protagonist very little or no time to solve their problems. This kind of time pressure forces the protagonist to consider options they wouldn't normally consider and to act without overthinking. The deadline (a specific time) or ticking clock (time pressure without a specific timeframe) are useful devices to add excitement in any story as long as they emerge organically from the setting and circumstances.

In *Harry Potter and the Sorcerer's Stone,* this kind of time pressure is highlighted in multiple instances. For example, in chapter sixteen, "Through the Trapdoor," we learn that Hagrid told a stranger in the pub how to get past the three-headed dog guarding the trapdoor on the third-floor corridor. This means it's only a matter of time until Snape (really, Quirrell) takes action. He now has everything he needs to get to the Sorcerer's Stone—except he still has to get past Dumbledore. A few pages later, we learn that Dumbledore has been called away from the castle, which means Snape (really, Quirrell) will most likely act *tonight* (deadline). Notice how the time pressure escalates and the deadline gets more specific over time. This is a fantastic way to up the stakes in an Action story—and it's an effective way to "force" your protagonist to grow and change.

3 - Set-Piece Action Sequences

Set-piece action sequences are mini-action stories within the global story. These scenes or groups of scenes move the story forward in a *significant* way, and they're often the larger, more exciting moments that your external plot and protagonist's internal arc pivot around. This is why they usually occur in or around the obligatory moments—and why they're often the most memorable scenes in a story.

This is also why set-piece action sequences can be challenging to write. They often require a lot of planning and layering to create something that moves both the external and internal storylines forward. You'll need to manage (and layer together) multiple plot lines, including subplots, to ensure the emotion of the set piece is building and hitting the intended emotional note (usually excitement) throughout the entire scene.

Harry Potter and the Sorcerer's Stone has quite a few set-piece action sequences, but my favorite occurs in chapter sixteen "Through the Trapdoor." In this penultimate chapter, Harry, Ron, and Hermione must successfully pass several challenges in order to retrieve the Sorcerer's Stone. They have to circumvent a ferocious three-headed dog, escape from the strangling tendrils of Devil's Snare, retrieve a flying key from among hundreds, win a life-sized game of wizard's chess, and finally master a riddle of poisonous potions before Harry can face Voldemort in that final chamber.

This scene is particularly fun because each of these challenges emphasizes a different magical skill, which corresponds to the Hogwarts professor who instituted the challenge. It also helps highlight Harry's strengths and weaknesses and shows why Harry, Ron, and Hermione are stronger together than apart. Harry, Ron, and Hermione each bring a different set of skills to this series of challenges. As first-year students, none of them have the magical experience or talent that would allow them to reach the Sorcerer's Stone on their own; they must help each other move from challenge to challenge.

I will highlight some of the other set-piece action sequences in this masterwork guide, but keep in mind that a set piece can be one scene or a sequence of scenes. And remember that in the Story Grid universe, we don't determine where a scene starts and ends solely based on a change in location or cast of characters. We're looking for a defined *and meaningful* value shift that impacts the global story as well as a change in the protagonist's scene goal.

When writing your own set-piece action sequences, keep in mind that whatever happens in these scenes needs to tangibly affect the outcome of the story—your plot and your character's development. It needs to alter the story's course of direction. It can't just be a flashy or exciting distraction simply to keep the reader entertained. That won't work. These set-piece action sequences must feel so integral to the storyline (and the reader's enjoyment) that they cannot be edited out of the final product.

Now, earlier I mentioned that these set-piece action sequences tend to happen in or around obligatory moments, so let's take a look at those next.

OBLIGATORY MOMENTS

Conventions set up conflicts. And from conflicts come changes in the global value from scene to scene and across the entire Action story arc. But where and when do these conflicts take place in the context of the story? How do they unfold, and how can you create the cause-and-effect pattern that a reader of Action story will recognize?

The answer comes in the form of obligatory moments. When the conventions of the Action genre are adhered to, certain situations tend to emerge organically. These are the unexpected events, revelations, decisions, and actions that help create change over the course of a story. These moments align with the Five Commandments of Storytelling and include the following:

- The Inciting Incident, which is an unexpected event that kicks off the action in the story or scene;
- The Turning Point Progressive Complication, which is an unexpected event or revelation that changes the global value in a significant way and gives rise to…
- The Crisis, which is a big question or dilemma that the protagonist must face in response to the Turning Point; and
- The Climax, which is the decision and action the protagonist takes in response to the Crisis

- The Resolution, which is the outcome of the action that happens in the Climax

Here's how those moments show up in *Harry Potter and the Sorcerer's Stone*:

Inciting Incident: Harry learns he's a wizard, and someone named Lord Voldemort tried to kill him when he was a baby. Also, there's a spot for him at Hogwarts School of Witchcraft and Wizardry where he can go to learn magic.

Note: Per the ACTION BEAT, the global Inciting Incident of an Action story should be "a life-threatening attack by the forces of antagonism." Although we don't see a literal "attack" by the antagonist in this scene, we *learn* about one that happened when Harry was a baby. This is a unique way to deliver on the global Inciting Incident of an Action story but with stakes appropriate for a middle-grade audience.

Turning Point Progressive Complication: After serving detention in the Forbidden Forest, Harry realizes that Voldemort is here and going after the Sorcerer's Stone.

Crisis: Should Harry try to stop Voldemort himself and risk his own life in the process? Or should he stay out of harm's way and let Voldemort come back to power just to kill him later?

Climax: Harry embraces his identity as The Boy Who Lived, and confronts Voldemort underneath the school.

Resolution: Harry defeats Voldemort and saves the Sorcerer's Stone.

Can you see the elements from the Action story framework at play here? Just by reading through the global Five Commandments, you can already get a sense of the core need (survival), the core value (life to death), the core event (hero at the mercy of the villain), and the core emotion (excitement). You can also see how the controlling idea (or theme) will be expressed based on the protagonist's journey from the global Inciting Incident to the Climax.

We can break this down even more by looking at the twenty skeletal scenes that unfold across each of the four quadrants. We call them skeletal scenes because they provide the structure for our stories. This is true of any story. But the nature of these events in an Action story is influenced by the genre's core need (survival) and core value (death-life). They're also influenced by Harry's internal Worldview arc that forces him to eventually embrace his identity as The Boy Who Lived.

Below, I've mapped out the first Harry Potter book using the twenty skeletal scenes of the Action Genre. It may seem that several important events have been left out, but remember, we're looking at the key moments in an Action story that move the plot and character arc forward. Of course, there's more to the story, but focusing on these significant moments of change allows us to think about the story as a whole and begin to consider the key scenes we need in our own stories, too. Let's take a look starting with the Beginning Hook.

TWENTY SKELETAL SCENES

Beginning Hook

The purpose of the Beginning Hook is to introduce the protagonist, their world, and the central conflict in such a way that readers are *hooked* and pulled into the rest of the story. This section includes the global Inciting Incident that threatens a need or provides an opportunity for the protagonist to get a need met (whether they consciously realize it or not). By the end of this section, the protagonist needs to (willingly or reluctantly) decide to engage with the central conflict, even if they don't fully understand the nature of the conflict just yet.

Let's take a look at how the Beginning Hook of *Harry Potter and the Sorcerer's Stone* works using the Five Commandments of Storytelling. To help us frame the conflict of this quadrant, the first thing we need to do is identify Harry's objective. Harry's objective is pretty simple. He just wants to stay off the Dursleys' radar to avoid making his life any worse than it already is. Let's take a look at the conflict that gets in the way of that goal and how this quadrant moves the story forward.

- **Inciting Incident:** The mail arrives with a letter addressed to Harry Potter in "The Cupboard under the Stairs," but the Dursleys won't let him have it.

- **Turning Point Progressive Complication:** Hagrid delivers Harry's letter (in person), which says he's a wizard and has been accepted into the Hogwarts School of Witchcraft and Wizardry. In the same conversation, Hagrid also tells Harry that his parents were murdered by the most powerful dark wizard of all time: Lord Voldemort.

- **Crisis:** After everything Harry's just learned from Hagrid, should he risk the unknown by going with him to Hogwarts? Or should he stay with the Dursleys to avoid the unknown?

- **Climax:** Harry decides to go to Hogwarts and travels with Hagrid to Diagon Alley to purchase school supplies. While there, Hagrid retrieves a mysterious package from Gringotts for Dumbledore, which Harry is *especially* curious about.

- **Resolution:** On September 1, Harry travels to King's Cross Station and boards the Hogwarts Express via Platform Nine and Three-Quarters.

As you can see, the arrival of the first letter addressed to Harry kicks off a chain of events that ultimately leads to Harry's decision to risk the unknown by going to Hogwarts. At the beginning of the quadrant, Harry had no idea what *really* happened to his parents or that he's famous in the wizarding world. By the end of the quadrant, he has *some* information but still doesn't know everything. He's starting to figure out who he is and what his place in the world looks like—even though this information gives rise to his inner obstacle. Although going to Hogwarts will inevitably result in a confrontation with Voldemort, the change in this quadrant *feels* positive. If Harry doesn't go to Hogwarts, he won't have the opportunity to learn magic, make friends, find somewhere to belong, and gain the confidence and skills needed to face and defeat Voldemort.

Middle Buildup

The purpose of the Middle Buildup is to show how the protagonist reacts to their new situation and to escalate (or *build up*) the conflict that was established in the Beginning Hook. Usually, the protagonist will attempt to deal with the external and internal conflict they face in this section by using skills and tactics that have served them in the past. So, although they're in a new situation, they're dealing with that new situation in an old way. That being said, they are *not* passive. They're still taking action, but their actions are usually *a response* (in one form or another) to what's happening around them. This section culminates with an event that raises the stakes (externally and internally) and forces the protagonist into a more *proactive* state.

Let's take a look at how the Middle Buildup of *Harry Potter and the Sorcerer's Stone* works using the Five Commandments of Storytelling. To help us frame the conflict of this quadrant, the first thing we need to do is identify Harry's objective. Harry's objective is to figure out where he belongs at Hogwarts (and in the wizarding world in general). Let's take a look at the conflict that gets in the way of that goal and how this quadrant moves the story forward.

- **Inciting Incident:** After the Sorting Ceremony, Harry's scar lights up in pain when he makes eye contact with a black-haired hooked-nose teacher (Snape).

- **Turning Point Progressive Complication:** While on their way to save Hermione from a giant troll, Harry and Ron see Snape heading for the third-floor corridor. Rather than follow him to find out what he's up to, Harry and Ron decide to help Hermione, and as a result, they become friends.

- **Crisis:** However, after accidentally eavesdropping on Snape discussing his injured leg with Filch, Harry makes the assumption that Snape let the troll into the castle so he could steal whatever the three-headed dog is guarding. Should he tell anyone about this information even if he might be wrong? Or keep it to himself?

- **Climax:** Although unable to shake the feeling that Snape's up to something, Harry does nothing. Instead, he shifts his focus to the upcoming Quidditch match in which someone jinxes his broom, almost killing him.

- **Resolution:** After the match, Harry, Ron, and Hermione talk to Hagrid about what happened. The kids are convinced Snape was the one who jinxed Harry's broom and tried to kill him, but Hagrid's not buying it. The kids also say they believe Snape's after what the three-headed dog is guarding, and Hagrid lets slip that whatever the dog is guarding has to do with Dumbledore and Nicolas Flamel, which offers the kids their first big clue about *what* is under the trapdoor.

A lot of good things happen to Harry in this quadrant. He gets sorted into Gryffindor, makes two really good friends, which is very important to Harry's success in the global climax, starts to learn magic, secures a spot on the Quidditch team, and even wins the first big match of the season. But ultimately, this quadrant shows a negative value shift for Harry. He's singled out by teachers and the other students because of his reputation as The Boy Who Lived, but he's yet to reconcile this legacy with himself. Shortly after encountering Professor Snape, Harry's goal shifts from figuring out where he belongs at Hogwarts to understanding why Professor Snape seems to dislike him so much.

This quest for understanding leads Harry into situations that raise question after question regarding the mysterious package hidden on the third floor. By the end of this quadrant, Harry has become the target of the antagonist, though he suspects the wrong person, and he's starting to understand what the antagonist wants—to steal whatever's hidden on the third floor. At this point, the stakes have been raised, and it's impossible for Harry to go back to how things were before the Quidditch match. Something bigger is going on at Hogwarts, and Harry and his friends are determined to get to the bottom of it. Luckily, Hagrid lets slip a really important clue. Whatever's hidden on the third floor has something to do with someone named Nicolas Flamel.

Middle Breakdown

The purpose of the Middle Breakdown is to show the protagonist reacting to the chaos that occurred in the climax of the previous section. By this point, they've usually had a revelation *about* the chaos, even if they can't put their revelation into concrete terms just yet. The central conflict is becoming clearer and clearer, but the protagonist still has no idea how they're going to solve the problem—especially since their internal obstacle is still (unknowingly) in their way. By the end of this section, the protagonist reaches an all-time low where they realize that in order to survive, they must take action—and that there are no guarantees when it comes to their survival.

Let's take a look at how the Middle Breakdown of *Harry Potter and the Sorcerer's Stone* works using the Five Commandments of Storytelling. To help us frame the conflict of this quadrant, the first thing we need to do is identify Harry's objective. Harry's objective is to figure out what Nicolas Flamel has to do with whatever's hidden on the third floor *so* he can figure out what Snape's up to. Let's take a look at the conflict that gets in the way of that goal and how this quadrant moves the story forward.

- **Inciting Incident:** Harry, Ron, and Hermione discover that Nicolas Flamel created the Sorcerer's Stone—a magical object that grants immortality. This must be what Snape wants and what's hidden on the third floor!

- **Turning Point Progressive Complication:** Harry, Ron, and Hermione help Hagrid relocate his baby dragon, but get detention and lose fifty points each for Gryffindor. This knocks Gryffindor out of the running for the championship and makes Harry wildly unpopular with his fellow Gryffindors. It also takes the wind out of his sails when it comes to finding out more about the Sorcerer's Stone.

- **Crisis:** But after overhearing someone threaten Quirrell, Harry assumes Quirrell told Snape how to get past the three-headed dog. Should Harry go to Dumbledore and risk getting into even more trouble? Or should he stay out of it and risk Snape getting his hands on the Sorcerer's Stone?

- **Climax:** Harry is determined to stay out of it until he comes across a hooded figure drinking unicorn blood while serving detention in the Forbidden Forest. On the way back to the castle, Firenze confirms the hooded figure is none other than Lord Voldemort himself.

- **Resolution:** Harry discusses everything that happened in the forest with his friends. They now assume Snape wants to steal the stone for Voldemort, and it's only a matter of time before Voldemort comes to finish him off.

After Hagrid lets slip that Nicolas Flamel has something to do with what's hidden on the third floor, Harry, Ron, and Hermione have their first big clue to work with. Harry's no longer just *reacting* to what's happening around him. He's *actively pursuing* the truth about the package and Snape's involvement. However, after Harry gets detention for helping Hagrid relocate Norbert and loses 150 points for Gryffindor, putting them in last place, he's essentially persona non grata. This takes the wind out of his sails, and he temporarily gives up his quest for the truth. But while serving detention, Harry gets his last big clue. Voldemort is here, at Hogwarts! It now appears that Snape has everything he needs to steal the Sorcerer's Stone for Voldemort, and there's no time to waste. Harry must act *now* if he wants to survive and stop Voldemort from coming back to full power.

Ending Payoff

The purpose of the Ending Payoff is to bring the protagonist and antagonist face to face in the global climax. Usually, the protagonist must join forces with others to succeed, and they must be willing to sacrifice (their safety, their agency, etc.) to increase the agency of the group and the survival of others. If the story has an internal arc, the protagonist must also overcome their internal obstacle and then demonstrate that they've done so in the global climax. By the end of this section, readers should have the answer to the question raised in the beginning hook, and if written correctly, they should feel the emotional payoff (core emotion) that's been promised since page one.

Let's take a look at how the Ending Payoff of *Harry Potter and the Sorcerer's Stone* works using the Five Commandments of Storytelling. To help us frame the conflict of this quadrant, the first thing we need to do is identify Harry's objective. Harry's objective is to prevent Snape from getting the Sorcerer's Stone from Voldemort. Let's take a look at the conflict that gets in the way of that goal and how this quadrant moves the story forward.

- **Inciting Incident:** After Hagrid confirms he told someone how to get past Fluffy, the kids run to tell Dumbledore what they know, but McGonagall informs them that Dumbledore has left the castle. Because of this, Harry assumes Snape will go after the stone tonight.

- **Turning Point Progressive Complication:** After navigating various dangerous obstacles underneath the school and losing Ron to a life-sized game of wizard's chess, Harry and Hermione realize they only have enough potion for one of them to go through to the final chamber.

- **Crisis:** Should Harry continue alone and face Snape/Voldemort alone with no backup? Or should he turn back and allow Voldemort to come back to full power, putting himself in danger anyway?

- **Climax:** Harry continues alone and comes face to face with Quirrell/Voldemort in the final chamber. Quirrell/Voldemort tries to use Harry to get the Sorcerer's Stone from the Mirror of Erised but fails.

- **Resolution:** Harry survives and has successfully prevented Voldemort from coming back to power.

After Hagrid confirms that he *did* tell someone how to get past Fluffy, the kids try to go to Dumbledore for help but learn that Dumbledore has been suspiciously called away on last-minute business, and no other adult is willing to believe them. Now, of course, Harry has to take action. Harry (and Ron and Hermione) demonstrate a great deal of courage, creativity and out-of-the-box thinking by sneaking past Fluffy, fighting their way out of Devil's Snare, catching the flying key, winning a life-sized (and life-threatening!) game of chess and choosing the correct potion. But notice that Rowling has Harry continue alone to the last room to face Quirrell and Voldemort. His friends cannot save him.

Ultimately, Harry and no one else can be the hero. In the climactic moment (core event), Voldemort offers Harry what he's always wanted—a life with his two loving (and deceased) parents *and* a future free of being The Boy Who Lived—in exchange for joining him on the dark side. If Harry hadn't learned how to accept his present life (a life without his parents) and his legacy, he wouldn't have been able to save the stone by looking in the mirror and seeing it appear in his pocket. Although this quadrant starts with Harry's life in immediate danger, it ends on the positive side of the life and death spectrum. Harry has successfully prevented Voldemort from getting the Sorcerer's Stone (although he's not confirmed dead), and Harry has saved himself and his friends from death, restoring their collective agency.

THE ACTION STORY UNDER THE MICROSCOPE

Now that we've talked about the Action story framework, the conventions and obligatory moments of an Action story, and the twenty skeletal scenes that provide the structure (or backbone) of the story it's time to see how these principles show up on a scene-by-scene basis.

Throughout the rest of this analysis guide, we're going to take a deep dive into each scene in this first Harry Potter book to see how the individual scenes add up to the global story. But to do so, let's make sure we're on the same page about what it means to write a scene.

Scenes are the building blocks of story and act like mini-stories of their own. They involve characters doing things (moving and speaking) in pursuit of a goal and in conflict with other characters or the nature of the environment. This conflict causes characters to act, and those actions cause change and come with consequences that move the story forward.

When we can identify the actions, conflict, change, and consequences in a scene, we can see the small decisions a writer like Rowling makes to build the bigger story. In our own stories, we can determine whether the scene is affecting the core value, life-death in an Action story, or whether the scene should be eliminated. We combine action, conflict, change, and consequences in a short, specialized summary we call the Story Event.

To be more precise, we say, a Story Event is an active change of a universal human value for one or more characters as a result of conflict.

One character's desires clash with another's, or an environmental shift changes the value positively or negatively.

A Working Scene contains at least one Story Event, and to determine a scene's Story Event, we answer four Socratic questions. You'll find my answers to these questions for every scene in *Harry Potter and the Sorcerer's Stone* following this introduction, but let's talk about them one by one first.

The first question is: **What are the characters literally doing—that is, what are their micro on-the-surface actions?**

We say this is what the characters are literally doing, but it also includes what they are saying. This is pretty straightforward and might include things like having a conversation, eating a meal, fighting a duel, or speaking to a crowd. It can also describe movement from location to location.

For example, in chapter five "Diagon Alley," Harry and Hagrid are traveling from the shack out at sea to London, through the Leaky Cauldron, and finally to Diagon Alley. Once there, they shop for Harry's school supplies. In other words, this on-the-surface action is how the characters traverse the scene or go about getting what they want, but it doesn't necessarily speak to their motivations or inner desires. That's the subject of the next question.

Character action evokes excitement in us because it's focused on how someone pursues what they want, which we can relate to, and is all about what is happening *now* in the story's present. Keep in mind the actions a character takes say a lot about who they are and what they believe. This is important for character and plot development.

The second question is: **What is the essential tactic of the characters— that is, what above-the-surface macro behaviors are they employing that are linked to a universal human value?**

As writers we can't just think about *what* the characters do. We also need to consider *why* they're doing it. This is what the "essential tactic" speaks to. What do the characters want in the scene? What's motivating them? Scenes require conflict, and that means characters must want different things. At least one active character in the scene must experience conflict (ideally from an antagonistic force) that prevents them from easily getting what they want. This desire at the scene level should align with what the character wants at the story level, which we call their conscious object of desire.

The external conflict in a scene can be anything—another character (or characters), the weather, a spell gone awry, mechanical failure, or whatever you want, really. The key thing to consider is how the external conflict puts pressure on your character's internal obstacle—or how it pushes their internal conflict to the surface and forces them to make decisions. These decisions cause change, which is the subject of the third question.

For example, in chapter five "Diagon Alley," Harry wants to gather all of his school supplies so he's ready to go to Hogwarts, but he's also eager to learn more about the wizarding world that he's now a part of. In this scene, he *does* face external conflict. He's not familiar with the world or how to navigate it, he meets Malfoy who he instantly dislikes, and everyone seems to have really high expectations of him, including Ollivander who says the world can expect great things from Harry. But he faces a lot of internal conflict in this scene, too. The more he interacts with the wizarding world, the more insecure he becomes. He's got a lot to learn, and he's not sure if he can live up to everyone's expectations of him.

In other words, the essential tactic is about what the character wants now and for the future and is based on how they see the world and themselves. We often pick this up between the lines of what's happening or in subtext. Characters don't always reveal their essential tactics because it could interfere with getting what they want when other characters oppose them. But it also serves a story purpose. Readers experience intrigue because they don't know (but want to know) why characters do what they do. This makes them keep reading to find out!

The third question is: **What beyond-the-surface universal human values have changed for one or more characters in the scene? Which one of those value changes is most important and should be included in the Story Grid Spreadsheet?**

The decisions characters make transform them and their situation. Each decision your character makes advances the plot, causing a change we can describe from positive to negative or vice versa. And when we talk about value and polarity shifts, this is what we mean. Think of universal human values as descriptive words used to explain how the main character(s) in the scene have changed, including their external circumstances or their internal condition from the beginning to the end of the scene.

For example, in chapter five "Diagon Alley," Harry successfully collects all of his school supplies. This positive shift enables him to go to Hogwarts, learn all the necessary spells, forge the all-important alliances, and develop the confidence and courage needed to face Voldemort in the end, even though he's feeling really insecure by the end of the scene. This scene also piques Harry's curiosity about the mysterious package Hagrid retrieves from vault 713. Although this curiosity puts Harry in danger, it's important that he feels called to investigate the package (and later protect it) because otherwise, Voldemort will succeed in coming back to power. Notice that Harry doesn't know any of this at the moment. For the purpose of this analysis, we view the scene from the perspective of knowing the entire story.

Now, one of the best ways to identify this shift is to look at the scene's Turning Point Progressive Complication. The Turning Point is the moment in a scene when the universal human value begins to shift, and it forces the character into the dilemma we call the Crisis. If you can identify those two points in a scene, it's usually much easier to identify the other structural elements.

The key point to remember is that the smaller scene-level changes must affect the global value, or the scene will distract from the story. A scene may include several value shifts, but that doesn't mean each one is indicative of "a scene." Multiple characters might even experience value shifts or changes in their situation—and those changes could be internal, external, or both. When you analyze a scene, the way you describe the changes and value shifts you see is up to you! Often, a shift is in the eye of the beholder, and it can be worded in a few different ways. What makes sense to one person may or may not make perfect sense to another. But when in doubt, focus on how the global value is enhanced or threatened, and you should be able to identify the important movement in any given scene.

Positive influences and actions result in desirable outcomes, like Harry's decision to ask the Sorting Hat to put him in any house but Slytherin in chapter seven, "The Sorting Hat," or his decision to save Hermione from the rogue troll in chapter ten, "Halloween." But his actions also result in self-sabotaging decisions like helping Hagrid relocate his baby dragon in chapter fourteen, "Norbert the Norwegian Ridgeback."

The variety of negative and positive shifts make the story engaging and push Harry forward in the story. The ups and downs allow readers to vicariously experience this emotional movement too. We see this in the scene-by-scene analysis, but you'll also be able to see it a bit more visually in the Story Grid Infographic that tracks Harry's external and internal journey from beginning to end.

The fourth and final question helps you synthesize your answers to the previous three questions and determine which value to enter on the Story Grid Spreadsheet. That question is: **What Story Event sums up the scene's on-the-surface actions, essential above-the-surface worldview behavioral tactics, and beyond-the-surface value change? We will enter that event in the Story Grid Spreadsheet.**

The Story Event is a short summary that brings the other three components together in a meaningful way. The Story Event does for the scene what a logline or controlling idea does for the entire story. It shows us what's important so we can immediately begin to see why the scene matters in the story. You could also say it answers the question: How does a character get closer to or further away from their story goal because of how they deal with the conflict they face on a scene-by-scene basis?

Crafting a Story Event can be intimidating, but it doesn't have to be! Don't be concerned if you feel confused or overwhelmed! Take your best guess and know there is no one single right answer. You can always make adjustments as you deepen your understanding of the story. Masterworks aren't analyzed in a day, and the skills needed to read critically like a writer will take time to develop as well. Luckily, you have this Masterwork Guide to help sharpen your analytical skills and help you write a story that works.

PUTTING IT ALL TOGETHER

Throughout this Masterwork Guide, I'm going to show you how Rowling constructed this story on a scene-by-scene basis. You'll see how each scene either moves Harry closer to life and safety or closer to death and danger. And if you're writing a middle-grade Action story, I want you to pay special attention to how the story doesn't include events across the entire range of values on the life and death spectrum. Rather, it saves life-or-death situations for the global Climax and peaks at Harry being "in danger" during significant plot events.

Your protagonist, like Harry, may never experience a fate worse than death. We know what that condition is for him, but he's not physically tortured in the story. That's appropriate for a younger audience and the questions explored in this story. In adult fiction, we spend a lot more time walking the line between death and a fate worse than death in part because that's the question we're exploring when we read that story. How do we keep going when we risk a fate worse than death in a horrific landscape?

You'll also see how the external plot events challenge Harry's inner obstacle on a scene-by-scene basis as well. You'll see how he develops friendships, learns to rely on his own inner compass, and finds the courage to stand up to the most powerful Dark Wizard in order to survive and keep his friends safe.

You'll also see how Rowling relied heavily on elements of the Crime genre (including things like clues and red herrings) to keep readers engaged in the story and to help pressure Harry to grow and change. Crime and Romance are two genres that make excellent subplots in Action Stories, and you'll see Rowling play with both throughout the Harry Potter series.

Now, a word of caution before we dive into the scene-by-scene analysis: Doing a close analysis of a masterwork, including a scene-by-scene breakdown of a favorite story, is a time-consuming, difficult, and highly subjective process. While you read through this guide—and as I share my thoughts on what advances the plot, how a character develops, or the value and polarity shift in each scene—know that this is *my* interpretation of why *Harry Potter and the Sorcerer's Stone* works, using the tools and terminology that Story Grid provides. It's okay if you disagree with my analysis or see things a little differently than I do. This doesn't mean that your interpretation of a scene (or of this story) is wrong. It also doesn't mean that my analysis is one hundred percent "right." As long as we agree on common terminology and an understanding of story principles, our individual analyses will most likely land us in the same spot, which is the most important part. I suggest you read this guide for the key takeaways (the *why* behind the *what*) versus getting too hung up on the nitty gritty details like which words I chose to describe a specific value shift or where exactly I chose to break a scene. So, with that being said, sit back, relax, and enjoy this breakdown of the first book in the Harry Potter series!

SCENE ANALYSIS

SCENE 1

THE BOY WHO LIVED

CHAPTER 1

2,042 words

"Mr. and Mrs. Dursley, of ... How very wrong he was."

Summary: Vernon Dursley hears and sees strange things on the way to work—a cat reading a map, people dressed in ridiculous cloaks, and even a mention of "The Potters" and "their son Harry." Rather than worry his wife, Petunia, Vernon keeps these observations to himself. He's confident that even if the Potters are involved in all this nonsense, there's no reason for them to bother him and his family.

ANALYZING THE SCENE

STORY EVENT

A Story Event is an active change of a universal human value for one or more characters as a result of conflict (one character's desires clash with another's, or an environmental shift changes the value positively or negatively).

A Working Scene contains at least one Story Event. To determine a scene's Story Event, answer these four Socratic questions:

1. **What are the characters literally doing—that is, what are their micro on-the-surface actions? Reader's Perspective (OTS)**

Mr. Dursley sees and hears strange things on his way to and from work. He watches the news and has dinner with his family.
OTS change (Mr. Dursley): Work to Home

2. **What is the essential tactic of the characters—that is, what above-the-surface macro behaviors are they employing that are linked to a universal human value? Character's Perspective (ATS)**

Mr. Dursley doesn't want the rumors he's hearing about "the Potters" and "their son Harry" to interfere with his family's ordinary life, so he ignores them. However, the wizarding world wants to celebrate! Somehow, baby Harry Potter just defeated Lord Voldemort, and they're elated!
ATS change (Mr. Dursley): Worried to Dismissive

3. **What beyond-the-surface universal human values have changed for one or more characters in the scene? Which one of those value changes is most important and should be included in the Story Grid Spreadsheet? Author's Perspective (BTS)**

Although Harry has just lost his parents, Voldemort has temporarily been defeated. While many wizards and witches celebrate this, nobody really knows what happened to Voldemort or whether he will or can return. For now, however, the wizarding world (including Harry) feels safe.
BTS change (Harry and the wizarding world): *Danger to Safety*

4. **The Scene Event Synthesis: What Story Event sums up the scene's on-the-surface, above-the-surface, and beyond-the-surface change? We will enter that event in the Story Grid Spreadsheet.**

As Vernon deals with strange events, the wizarding world celebrates Harry's survival and the (temporary) defeat of Lord Voldemort.

HOW THE SCENE ABIDES BY THE FIVE COMMANDMENTS OF STORYTELLING

Inciting Incident: Coincidental. Vernon sees a cat reading a map outside his home.

Turning Point Progressive Complication: Active. Mr. Dursley hears a stranger mention the Potter family and their son Harry.

Crisis: Best Bad Choice. Should Mr. Dursley tell Petunia he heard someone mention "the Potters" and "their son Harry"? Or should he shoulder the burden of worry himself and not upset Petunia any further?

Climax: Mr. Dursley doesn't tell Petunia anything specific.

Resolution: Despite everything he's seen and heard today—and that Petunia confirmed her nephew's name is, in fact, Harry—Mr. Dursley falls asleep feeling confident that anything to do with the Potters is unlikely to affect him and his family.

NOTES

- This one of two scenes in the story written entirely from the perspective of an omniscient narrator following a character other than Harry Potter. This was a necessary choice because, at this point in the story, Harry is barely a year old and his viewpoint is limited. It's interesting that you can have a scene following a secondary character, in this case Vernon Dursley, that still demonstrates a value shift for the protagonist. This is a creative way for us writers to deliver scenes that affect the

protagonist (and touch on the global story) even if the protagonist can't be present for one reason or another.
- This is the day Vernon's life starts to change. Seeing this scene unfold from Vernon's perspective helps us understand why he dislikes Harry so much and, eventually, why he blames Harry for his unhappiness, even if we don't agree with his way of thinking.
- By introducing strange and unusual things in this first scene, Rowling has let the reader know what kind of story they can expect *without* overwhelming them with world-building details. Because this story was meant for middle-grade readers, it has a shallow learning curve. A "learning curve" describes how long it takes a reader to get up to speed on the nuances of a story world. This is one of the many reasons it's important to know the age range of your target audience—so you can make decisions on things like your story's learning curve and how much information you'll give readers in opening chapters.
- By starting Harry's story here (versus another chapter like chapter two, "The Vanishing Glass"), Rowling introduces us to Harry in a moment of vulnerability. The troubled world he was born into has just been saved, but his own life has been destroyed. We develop a bond of empathy with Harry, knowing his new life with the Dursleys will not suit him. This tragic start along with the promise of a magical world provides an allure readers can't resist.
- Mr. Dursley's goal in this scene is to go to work, and he expects to have a normal day. The moment the conflict kicks into gear (when he sees the cat reading the map), his new goal is essentially to *ignore* the strangeness—even after he realizes that whatever's happening in the world could threaten his family's sense of normalcy (and the secret that he and Petunia are so keen to protect). Consider how this scene wouldn't have been as impactful if we didn't understand his goal and expectations. This is why it's crucial for us writers to understand (and communicate) what our point-of-view characters want in every

single scene. Their goals and expectations help us frame and give context to the conflict.
- Notice the tone of this opening scene. The author uses phrases like "perfectly normal, thank you," and "didn't hold with such nonsense." This helps readers *feel* how the Dursleys see and interact with the world. They believe they're better than everyone else and above it all. This is also a great example of how you can exemplify voice regardless of point of view choice.
- The cat Mr. Dursley sees outside of their house is none other than Professor McGonagall, which we learn in the next scene. This is a great setup for the next scene *and* later books in the series, where the ability of wizards to transform into animals becomes important to the plot (specifically in book three, *Harry Potter and the Prisoner of Azkaban*).
- This scene contains the very first mention of "You-Know-Who." We don't know why everyone is celebrating the fact that he's disappeared, but clearly, it's a big deal! This makes us curious about what happened and we wonder who "You-Know-Who" is, so we read forward to find out. Luckily, Rowling gives us some (but not all) of the answers in chapter four, "The Keeper of the Keys."
- This is also the first time that readers hear the term "Muggle." We don't know what it means yet, but we can infer that this divide between Muggles and magic users is important in this world and for these characters, especially if they've come up with names to describe the different groups. Prejudice is a theme Rowling touches on often in the Harry Potter books, and she's introducing us to a key term that will enable her to demonstrate the effects of prejudice throughout the book and series. First, we get a glimpse of Vernon's prejudice toward people who aren't like him. Then she deepens it once we get into the wizarding world and pays it off throughout the series with the overarching conflict Voldemort creates.
- Fun fact: Did you notice the newscaster's name is Ted? It's rumored that Ted Tonks is the newscaster mentioned in this scene.

- In this scene, Hagrid carries baby Harry to his new life in the Muggle World (Privet Drive). Later, in the last chapter "The Flaw in the Plan" of *Harry Potter and the Deathly Hallows,* Hagrid carries Harry's "dead" body up to the castle. Writers can use this technique to frame their stories—whether that be a series of stories, an individual book in the series, or a chapter within one of those books—and it evokes a feeling of satisfaction and completion in the reader when they realize everything's connected, even some of the small details!

SCENE 2
THE BOY WHO LIVED
CHAPTER 1

2,539 words

"Mr. Dursley might have been ... Potter — The Boy Who Lived!"

Summary: Later that night, Albus Dumbledore, the headmaster of Hogwarts School of Witchcraft and Wizardry, meets Professor McGonagall outside of the Dursleys' home. He confirms all the rumors are true. Voldemort killed Lily and James Potter and then disappeared after he failed to kill their son Harry. And not only that, but Voldemort's powers seem to be gone or broken as well. Dumbledore tells McGonagall of his plans to leave baby Harry with the Dursleys. She begs him to reconsider because they seem like horrible people, but Dumbledore has already made up his mind. He will leave Harry with the Dursleys to give him the best chance at a normal life. Hagrid arrives with baby Harry, and Dumbledore leaves Harry on the doorstep with a note imploring the Dursleys to take him in.

ANALYZING THE SCENE

STORY EVENT

A Story Event is an active change of a universal human value for one or more characters as a result of conflict (one character's desires clash with another's, or an environmental shift changes the value positively or negatively).

A Working Scene contains at least one Story Event. To determine a scene's Story Event, answer these four Socratic questions:

1. What are the characters literally doing—that is, what are their micro on-the-surface actions? Reader's Perspective (OTS)

Albus Dumbledore and Professor McGonagall talk while waiting for Hagrid to drop off baby Harry Potter. Dumbledore fills McGonagall in on his plans.

OTS change (Dumbledore): Hogwarts to Privet Drive

2. What is the essential tactic of the characters—that is, what above-the-surface macro behaviors are they employing that are linked to a universal human value? Character's Perspective (ATS)

Dumbledore wants to protect Harry and keep him safe. He also wants Harry to have a chance at a normal life, away from the spotlight and the inevitable fame that comes with being The Boy Who Lived, so he leaves Harry with the Dursleys. However, Professor McGonagall also wants to protect Harry, but she doesn't trust the Dursleys. She thinks Harry should grow up in the wizarding world instead of the Muggle world but ultimately trusts Dumbledore's judgment.

ATS change (Dumbledore): Friendly to Firm / Resistance to Compliance

3. What beyond-the-surface universal human values have changed for one or more characters in the scene? Which one of those value changes

is most important and should be included in the Story Grid Spreadsheet? Author's Perspective (BTS)

Though Dumbledore knows the Durselys aren't the best kind of people, he also knows Harry will be protected while growing up here, mainly due to the charm he placed on Harry that we don't learn about until later in the series. So, although Harry will have to live in an unpleasant home (with unpleasant people), he is ultimately much safer growing up here with family.

BTS change (Harry): *Unprotected to Protected*

4. The Scene Event Synthesis: What Story Event sums up the scene's on-the-surface, above-the-surface, and beyond-the-surface change? We will enter that event in the Story Grid Spreadsheet.

Dumbledore drops Harry off at the Dursleys' home so he can grow up safe and well outside of the wizarding world.

HOW THE SCENE ABIDES BY THE FIVE COMMANDMENTS OF STORYTELLING

Inciting Incident: Causal. McGonagall is waiting outside the Dursleys' home.

Turning Point Progressive Complication: Active. McGonagall challenges Dumbledore's plans, stating that the Dursleys are not appropriate guardians.

Crisis: Best Bad Choice. Should Dumbledore stick to his plan despite McGonagall's hesitations? Or should he change his plans based on McGonagall's observations?

Climax: Dumbledore remains firm on his plans but explains his reasoning to McGonagall.

Resolution: Hagrid arrives with baby Harry, and they leave him on the Dursleys' doorstep. Dumbledore, Professor McGonagall, and Hagrid are all sad to leave Harry but confident that they've made the best decision for his future.

NOTES

- Notice that although this scene has a similar value shift as scene one, (danger to safety and unprotected to protected) this scene offers a different emotional experience for readers. From the perspective of the reader, we track Mr. Dursley in scene one, and we can't help but feel his worry over the strange events happening around him. In scene two, we are left with a more positive feeling of hope for Harry's future. In this way, Rowling was able to deliver two scenes, back-to-back, with a similar feeling value shift, but the reader experiences them in different ways. This is a wonderful strategy to put in your own writing toolbox, especially when considering which scenes to combine into a chapter.
- Dumbledore's goal in this scene is to leave Harry with the Dursleys so he can grow up without the potential negative effects of fame. However, fame will be something Harry has to deal with throughout the series regardless. The humility Harry learns will become one of his greatest strengths, and it's largely due to this decision Dumbledore makes on his behalf. This quality will separate him from Voldemort and will define him throughout the series. Even now, Dumbledore suspects that a piece of Voldemort lives inside Harry and will likely grow stronger as Harry ages, so creating opportunities that will help Harry grow into someone who is *unlike* Voldemort and can make different choices than Voldemort is one of the best things he can do for Harry. In this way, Dumbledore is the ultimate (yet imperfect) mentor, always acting with Harry's best interest in mind.

- Dumbledore uses the "Put-Outer," later called the Deluminator, which ends up being gifted to Ron Weasley in *Harry Potter and the Deathly Hallows*. This tool is one of Dumbledore's genius inventions and pays off in significant ways throughout the series.
- McGonagall mentions that Dumbledore is the only one Voldemort has ever feared. This is a great hint at Dumbledore and Voldemort's history that we only start learning about in *Harry Potter and the Half-Blood Prince*. That being said, notice there is *not* a ton of backstory about Dumbledore and Voldemort included on the page. Instead, Rowling only included what readers *need to know* to make sense of the scene. What little information she reveals keeps the reader guessing and evokes that sense of mystery that readers love. This is exactly the way to think about which backstory details to include (or exclude) in your own scenes and stories.
- Hagrid arrives on Sirius Black's motorcycle. This is the first mention of Sirius Black, who becomes a prominent character in book three, *Harry Potter and the Prisoner of Azkaban* (and the series). The fact that Sirius generously let Hagrid borrow his motorcycle to deliver Harry to the Dursleys is such a small detail that most readers will forget it by the time they read book three. This allows Rowling to use Sirius as a red herring (in book three) while still providing clues to Sirius's true nature from the start.
- Notice how the small mention of Madam Pomfrey gives readers the illusion of a much bigger story world *without* a ton of explanation or backstory. We'll meet her later, but we don't need to know who she is or what she does for the scene to make sense.
- Dumbledore says he would trust Hagrid with his life. This is a great setup of Hagrid's character. He doesn't always do the right thing, but he has good intentions and is one of the most loyal characters in the series. We trust Hagrid and give him the benefit of the doubt because Dumbledore does. Consider how this lays the foundation for how we interpret Hagrid's behavior

and decisions later on in the story when it seems he's keeping secrets and making less than ideal decisions.
- Rowling mentions the word "Muggles" again in this scene—and now, we have a slightly better understanding of what it means. Because she introduces the term with more context each time, she's essentially teaching us the language of her world as we read forward.
- Dumbledore is eating lemon drops in this scene, and later, "lemon drops" becomes the password to get into his office. This might seem like a throwaway detail at first glance, but instead, it's a great way to show readers what Dumbledore's personality is like. He's a fun, playful, and sometimes whimsical guy! When writing your own stories, consider how even small details like this can make an impression on readers—but don't expect to have all the details figured out while writing your first draft. This is likely something Rowling developed and sharpened through the revision process.
- Did you notice that Dumbledore doesn't want to remove Harry's scar because "scars can come in handy?" This turns out to be true because, throughout the series, Harry's scar serves as a warning sign that Voldemort is near. It also represents a link between Harry and Voldemort that will be exposed in later books.
- Fun Fact: Did you know that Harry's scar is lightning-shaped because of how you perform the Avada Kedavra spell? This is a great example of how Rowling makes every little detail count. Did she have this planned out before writing the series? Probably not. For many writers, these types of connections tend to appear during revisions and/or while writing later books.

SCENE 3

THE VANISHING GLASS

CHAPTER 2

3,439 words

"Nearly ten years had passed ... to disagree with Dudley's gang."

Summary: Ten years later, Harry lives in a cupboard underneath the stairs at the Dursleys' house. It's Dudley's birthday and the family, including Harry, head to the zoo. In the reptile house, the boa constrictor winks at Harry and they strike up a conversation. Somehow, Dudley and his friend Piers end up behind the glass enclosure while the snake escapes. Mr. Dursley blames Harry and sends him to his cupboard with no meals.

ANALYZING THE SCENE

STORY EVENT

A Story Event is an active change of a universal human value for one or more characters as a result of conflict (one character's desires clash with another's, or an environmental shift changes the value positively or negatively).

A Working Scene contains at least one Story Event. To determine a scene's Story Event, answer these four Socratic questions:

1. What are the characters literally doing—that is, what are their micro on-the-surface actions? Reader's Perspective (OTS).

The Dursleys and Harry celebrate Dudley's birthday with a visit to the zoo.
OTS change (Harry): Privet Drive to the Zoo

2. What is the essential tactic of the characters—that is, what above-the-surface macro behaviors are they employing that are linked to a universal human value? Character's Perspective (ATS).

Harry wants to have a good time at the zoo. The Dursleys want Dudley to have a good birthday, and in order for that to happen, they need Harry to uphold their expectations of no "funny business."
ATS change (Harry): Hopeful to Hopeless

3. What beyond-the-surface universal human values have changed for one or more characters in the scene? Which one of those value changes is most important and should be included in the Story Grid Spreadsheet? Author's Perspective (BTS)

Harry's ability to talk to the snake and unconsciously cause the glass to vanish confirms Vernon and Petunia's ultimate fear. Despite trying to "stamp it out of him," Harry has magic, just like his "freakish" mother. Harry, not knowing he's a wizard, worries that his oddities will make the Dursleys treat him even worse than they do now. Until Harry has contact with the wizarding world and fully learns to understand his powers, his abilities get him in trouble with his aunt and uncle, which leads to undesirable living conditions.
BTS Change (Harry): *Hidden to Exposed*

4. The Scene Event Synthesis: What Story Event sums up the scene's on-

the-surface, above-the-surface, and beyond-the-surface change? We will enter that event in the Story Grid Spreadsheet.

Harry communicates with a boa constrictor at the zoo and accidentally traps Dudley in the snake pit, which exposes his gifts and infuriates the Dursleys even more than usual.

HOW THE SCENE ABIDES BY THE FIVE COMMANDMENTS OF STORYTELLING

Inciting Incident: Causal. Mrs. Figg can't babysit Harry because she broke her leg.

Turning Point Progressive Complication: Action. Harry suggests they leave him home alone.

Crisis: Best Bad Choice. Should the Dursleys bring Harry to the zoo and risk ruining Dudley's birthday? Or should they leave him home unsupervised and risk coming home to find the house in ruins?

Climax: The Dursleys decide to bring Harry with them to the zoo.

Resolution: Harry can't believe his luck! All goes well at the zoo until Harry talks to a boa constrictor and (unknowingly) releases it from the enclosure. The Dursleys are so upset that they send Harry to his "room" (the cupboard under the stairs) with no meals.

NOTES

- It's been ten years since Dumbledore left Harry at the Dursleys, which means we're dipping into Harry's life right before he turns eleven years old. This is significant because young wizards get their letter to Hogwarts on their eleventh birthday. Had Rowling not started the main story here (excluding chapter one, which is more like a prologue in disguise), we wouldn't have had the appropriate amount of time to get to know Harry, see his miserable life, and understand what's currently lacking for him. At the same time, action *does* happen in this scene. It's not simply a day-in-the-life of an eleven-year-old boy who lives in a cupboard underneath the stairs.

- Although this chapter spans multiple locations, I analyzed it as one scene because there is one major value shift. The first part of the scene revolves around the conflict the Dursleys face when Mrs. Figg cancels. They face a crisis. Will they bring Harry to the zoo or risk leaving him unsupervised? Even though Harry doesn't own the main scene crisis, the Dursleys' decision to bring Harry to the zoo creates a situation and circumstances that impact Harry. This is the key to creating a crisis moment that belongs to another character yet impacts the protagonist and touches on the global story. When Harry talks to the snake and (unknowingly) releases it from the enclosure, there's more of an implied crisis from Harry's perspective, or a crisis that isn't one hundred percent on the page. Harry doesn't know how to use magic, but since it's a part of him, he's able to use it almost instinctively in his (and the snake's) defense. If so much weight wasn't given to the Dursleys' decision to bring Harry to the zoo, and if the stakes weren't set up during that decision, the second half of this scene would likely fall flat.
- Harry says Dudley looks like a "pig in a wig," and later, in chapter four, "The Keeper of the Keys," Hagrid gives Dudley a curly pig's tail. This is a fun way to reinforce Dudley's appearance and mannerisms. We can't help but imagine Dudley to be rather piggish after these back-to-back descriptions.
- Did you notice how Rowling is still slowly introducing strange things scene by scene? Here, we're introduced to the idea of humans talking to snakes. Harry being a Parselmouth plays a big part in book two, *Harry Potter and the Chamber of Secrets,* but we

don't need to know or understand this detail yet. It also shows that Harry is capable of magic and that his capabilities are increasing. Strange things have happened around Harry before, such as getting a haircut only to have his hair grow back overnight, a sweater shrinking simply because Harry didn't want to wear it, and being found on the roof of the school kitchens after being chased by Dudley's gang—but nothing *this* drastic has ever happened before. If Rowling dumped all of this on us at once, it would be overwhelming, and we'd focus more on world-building than connecting with Harry.

- Rowling mentions a few more tertiary characters here—Mrs. Figg and Aunt Marge. The time and attention spent describing Harry's relationship with Mrs. Figg suggests she's more than just a neighbor, but we don't know the full extent of her role in Harry's world until book five, *Harry Potter and the Order of the Phoenix*. Aunt Marge, on the other hand, is only briefly mentioned. She *will* show up later in book three, *Harry Potter and the Prisoner of Azkaban,* but overall holds a less significant role than Mrs. Figg. If you're writing a series, you don't have to know *every single* purpose your tertiary characters will serve throughout the series—especially when writing book one—but it can be a great exercise to compare how much page time a tertiary character gets versus their importance to the story you're currently writing and the series as a whole.
- On a similar note, Harry recalls how sometimes strangers in the street seem to know him, such as the tiny man in a violet top hat that bowed to him while shopping with the Dursleys. Harry meets this man (Dedalus Diggle) in chapter five, "Diagon Alley," when Hagrid takes him through the Leaky Cauldron in London. We can only guess at whether Rowling planned this connection from the start or made the connection later while revising, but it's a fun detail that makes the story (and world) feel more cohesive and real.
- Harry mentions having dreamed of a flying motorcycle (Hagrid delivering him to the Dursleys) as well as seeing a blinding flash

of green light and feeling a burning pain in his forehead (Voldemort's killing curse). Even though we don't fully understand these details yet, they hint at what happened the night Harry's parents were killed. Rowling could have had Harry dream about *anything*, but she pulled from the plot and his backstory to make his dreams more significant.

SCENE 4

THE LETTERS FROM NO ONE

CHAPTER 3

3,526 words

"The escape of the Brazilian ... cheer him up at all."

Summary: It's now summer vacation, and Harry is looking forward to the start of the new school year if only so he can spend time away from Dudley. One day, the mail arrives with a letter addressed to Harry Potter who lives in "The Cupboard under the Stairs." Harry is excited to receive mail, but before he can read the letter, Uncle Vernon takes it away. More and more letters arrive for Harry over the next few days, and Vernon is so furious about this that he decides to take his family somewhere more remote—first the Railview Hotel and later the shack out at sea—where the letters can't reach them.

ANALYZING THE SCENE

STORY EVENT

A Story Event is an active change of a universal human value for one or more characters as a result of conflict (one character's desires clash with another's, or an environmental shift changes the value positively or negatively).

A Working Scene contains at least one Story Event. To determine a scene's Story Event, answer these four Socratic questions:

1. What are the characters literally doing—that is, what are their micro on-the-surface actions? Reader's Perspective (OTS).

Petunia is sorting Harry and Dudley's clothing for the upcoming school year while Vernon reads the paper. When the mail arrives with a letter addressed to Harry, Vernon prevents Harry from receiving the sender's message.

OTS change (Harry): Privet Drive to Railview Hotel to the shack out at sea / Home to Away

2. What is the essential tactic of the characters—that is, what above-the-surface macro behaviors are they employing that are linked to a universal human value? Character's Perspective (ATS).

Harry wants to read the letters and to figure out who's trying to contact him because he's never received a piece of mail before. Vernon doesn't want anyone to contact Harry, especially anyone in the wizarding world, so he does not allow Harry to read the letters. The mysterious sender of the letters wants Harry to receive them because it's almost the start of term, so they continue sending them relentlessly.

ATS change (Harry): Feeling Seen to Lonely

3. What beyond-the-surface universal human values have changed for one or more characters in the scene? Which one of those value changes

is most important and should be included in the Story Grid Spreadsheet? Author's Perspective (BTS).

Harry's Hogwarts letter is an invitation to safety (because being able to train as a wizard will prepare him to go against Voldemort) but also a better life (because he will be with people who are like him and who will love him for who he is). As long as the Dursleys succeed in preventing Harry from getting his Hogwarts letter, Harry (unknowingly) runs the risk of not being adequately prepared to face Voldemort when he eventually comes calling. In other words, if Harry doesn't learn the truth about himself and go to Hogwarts, he won't gain the confidence, skills, and allies needed to face and defeat Voldemort.

BTS change (Harry): *Potential for Safety to Potential for Safety Threatened*

4. The Scene Event Synthesis: What Story Event sums up the scene's on-the-surface, above-the-surface, and beyond-the-surface change? We will enter that event in the Story Grid Spreadsheet.

Mr. Dursley intercepts a swarm of letters that arrive for Harry, and in order to prevent Harry from reading them, he moves the family to a remote island.

HOW THE SCENE ABIDES BY THE FIVE COMMANDMENTS OF STORYTELLING

Inciting Incident: Causal. The post arrives with a letter addressed to Harry Potter in "The Cupboard under the Stairs."

Turning Point Progressive Complication: Action. The post arrives with more letters for Harry even though it's Sunday and there's no post on Sunday.

Crisis: Best Bad Choice. Should Vernon stay home and continue to intercept the letters? Or should he take his family away from the house so the sender can't reach Harry?

Climax: Vernon takes the family away from the house.

Resolution: The family goes to the Railview Hotel, but the letters for Harry still arrive. Desperate to escape the letters, Vernon takes his family to a remote shack out at sea. He's thrilled, thinking he finally escaped the mysterious letter-sender, but Harry is miserable.

NOTES

- This is the Inciting Incident of the Beginning Hook, threatening both Harry's safety and worldview. Someone is trying to get in touch with him, but he has no friends or family. So who could it be? Uncle Vernon and Aunt Petunia seem to know who's trying to contact Harry, and it's clear that they don't want Harry to know anything about it. This raises the question in the mind of the reader (and Harry), "Who is trying to contact Harry? Why? What do the Dursleys know that Harry doesn't?" We'll learn the answers to these questions as we read through the rest of the Beginning Hook.
- This scene is a great example of how writers can play with literal value shifts (Harry being freezing and miserable in the shack out at sea threatens his safety) as well as not so literal value shifts (Harry won't be prepared to face Voldemort if he doesn't go to Hogwarts, which also threatens his safety). This is why it's important to consider all the different perspectives (author BTS, character ATS, and reader OTS), especially when revising!
- There's a lot of proof of how horrible Harry's life is in this chapter. He spends a ton of time trying to figure out how to avoid Dudley's gang, he's going to a local public school while Dudley's going to a private school, and he's getting Dudley's dyed hand-me-downs to wear for the new school year. As readers, we can't help but root for Harry's life to improve by the end of the book. And this type of "rooting interest" deepens the

empathy we already feel for Harry coming out of chapters one and two.
- The purple wax seal on the envelope gives us the first hint at the Hogwarts School houses—a coat of arms showing a lion, an eagle, a badger, and a snake surrounding a large letter *H*. We don't know what this means yet, but we don't have to! Details like this serve to pique our curiosity and get us excited about what's to come.

SCENE 5

THE KEEPER OF THE KEYS

CHAPTER 4

3,995 words

"As night fell, the promised ... in one o' the pockets."

Summary: At midnight, Harry turns eleven just as a giant (Hagrid) knocks down the door of the shack. Once inside, and despite *a lot* of protesting by the Dursleys, Hagrid tells Harry he's a wizard, and he's been accepted to Hogwarts School of Witchcraft and Wizardry. Term starts on September 1! Later, Hagrid tells Harry that You-Know-Who (Voldemort) killed his parents, and that Voldemort tried to kill Harry, too, but failed, which led to Voldemort's downfall. Harry has a hard time believing all of this and even tells Hagrid he's made a mistake, but Hagrid convinces Harry it's all true.

ANALYZING THE SCENE

STORY EVENT

A Story Event is an active change of a universal human value for one or more characters as a result of conflict (one character's desires clash with

another's, or an environmental shift changes the value positively or negatively).

A Working Scene contains at least one Story Event. To determine a scene's Story Event, answer these four Socratic questions:

1. What are the characters literally doing—that is, what are their micro on-the-surface actions? Reader's Perspective (OTS)

Hagrid arrives at the shack and has a conversation with Harry and the Dursleys.
OTS change (Harry): Alone (With the Dursleys) to Companioned (By Hagrid)

2. What is the essential tactic of the characters—that is, what above-the-surface macro behaviors are they employing that are linked to a universal human value? Character's Perspective (ATS)

Hagrid wants to escort Harry to Hogwarts per Dumbledore's instructions, but must get through the Dursleys to do so. Harry wants to learn the truth about himself and his parents because he's lived with unanswered questions for eleven years, but Vernon and Petunia don't want Harry to know the truth because they don't like anything to do with magic.
ATS change (Harry): Hopeless to Hopeful

3. What beyond-the-surface universal human values have changed for one or more characters in the scene? Which one of those value changes is most important and should be included in the Story Grid Spreadsheet? Author's Perspective (BTS)

Harry learns some big truths in this scene. He's a wizard, he's been accepted to a magical boarding school, and someone named Voldemort killed his parents. This very big moment kicks off his internal Worldview arc. Even though he's moving one step closer to an inevitable confrontation with Voldemort (danger), this is the first time he's ever come face to face with his true identity (knowledge). By embracing his role in the wizarding world and by taking his place at Hogwarts, he'll be more equipped to handle Voldemort when the time to face him comes. However, he'll face escalating danger along the way first.

BTS change (Harry): *Ignorance to Knowledge*

4. **The Scene Event Synthesis: What Story Event sums up the scene's on-the-surface, above-the-surface, and beyond-the-surface change? We will enter that event in the Story Grid Spreadsheet.**

Hagrid arrives at the shack and tells Harry what was in the letter and what really happened to his parents before escorting him to Hogwarts.

HOW THE SCENE ABIDES BY THE FIVE COMMANDMENTS OF STORYTELLING

Inciting Incident: Causal. A giant barges in through the front door of the shack.

Turning Point Progressive Complication: Revelation. Hagrid tells Harry that he's a wizard, and he's been accepted into Hogwarts School of Witchcraft and Wizardry.

Crisis: Irreconcilable Goods Choice. Should Harry go to Hogwarts and risk the unknown? Or should Harry listen to the Dursleys and remain somewhere familiar?

Climax: Harry agrees to go to Hogwarts.

Resolution: Harry feels both nervous and excited about the future.

NOTES

- This is the global Inciting Incident of the story *and* the Turning Point and Crisis of the Beginning Hook. In this scene, Harry learns the truth about who he is and what happened to his parents. This helps Harry have more of a sense of his own identity. He had parents who were magical and loved, which establishes a legacy for Harry to live up to. We also see that, despite how he's felt for the last eleven years, he *does* belong somewhere—the wizarding world! This *feels* good to Harry and the reader. But by learning all of this and agreeing to go to Hogwarts, Harry is actually moving one step closer to inevitable danger. If he goes to Hogwarts, he'll eventually face Voldemort over the Sorcerer's Stone. This scene is an excellent example of how to cross the external genre of the story with the internal genre in an impactful and unforgettable way.

- As the Inciting Incident of the global story, this sets up the global Climax. Although we don't see a literal "attack" by the antagonist, we *learn* about one that happened when Harry was a baby. This is a unique way to deliver on the global Inciting Incident of an Action story but with stakes appropriate for a middle-grade audience. It also addresses major questions that challenge Harry's internal arc and inner obstacle: Will Harry come face to face with Voldemort again? Does he have what it takes to live up to his reputation? Will he eventually step into his identity as The Boy Who Lived? Herein lies the lesson of the entire series, too. Everyone is worthy, regardless of circumstance. And with love and friendship, everyone is capable of becoming who they were meant to be.

- Notice that Hagrid performs magic using his umbrella but then later admits he was expelled from Hogwarts in his third year. This small detail piques our curiosity. How can he do magic if he was expelled from Hogwarts? In book two, *Harry Potter and the Chamber of Secrets*, we learn more about Hagrid's backstory, and Harry suspects that Dumbledore fashioned Hagrid's wand into the pink umbrella after he was expelled. Did Rowling have all of this figured out while writing book one? Maybe, maybe not. This is a great example of something that *could* have been just a fun detail but later was turned into something more significant when fleshing out Hagrid's backstory. Who knows! When writing a series, we can't put too much pressure on ourselves to come up with small details like this that will hold significance later. All we can do is focus on crafting a story that works *and then* forge the connections between details (or develop those details and connections) later.

- Hagrid shows Harry kindness in multiple ways in this scene. Unlike the Dursleys, Hagrid's willing to answer Harry's questions and, in doing so, provides the first real link to Lily and James. This is huge for an eleven-year-old who has never felt that connection to his parents! Hagrid even tells Harry he looks like his parents and that he has his mother's eyes. This is a huge setup that pays off later on in the series, especially in book six, *Harry Potter and the Half-Blood Prince*. Harry will often be told he has his mother's eyes, and this plays a big part in Harry's relationship with Snape throughout the series. All of this further cements Hagrid's place as the "good guys" for Harry and readers.

- This scene takes place on July 31, Harry's birthday. This is significant because it's the main reason Lord Voldemort targeted Harry and killed his parents. Voldemort learned of a prophecy about a boy born in late July who would lead to his downfall, so he sought out the Potter family, killed Lily and James, and tried but failed to kill young Harry. It's interesting that Rowling chose to start each of the Harry Potter books before or on Harry's birthday because birthdays are relatable milestones for middle-grade readers. In this way, Rowling helps build the connection between readers and Harry (whether inadvertently or on purpose).

- Hagrid says that some people believe Voldemort is still out there, "bidin' his time." It's clear that people fear Voldemort's return, which sets up the stakes for this book and the rest of the series. In the same conversation, Hagrid mentions that Dumbledore is the only person Voldemort fears, which echoes what McGonagall said in chapter one. By including details like this more than once, Rowling ensures we understand the

dynamic between Dumbledore and Voldemort (and the stakes) right from the start.
- Aunt Petunia confirms that she and Vernon knew that Harry was a wizard and that his parents were, too. This raises questions for the reader. What else do the Dursleys know? Does this have something to do with the letter Dumbledore left in the basket with baby Harry back in chapter one? We don't learn the answer to these questions in book one, but we do learn more about Petunia's backstory throughout the series.
- Notice how slowly Rowling is introducing the world-building details to both readers and Harry. In this scene, we learn a little bit more about the world. There's a place called Hogwarts that only admits witches and wizards, dark wizards do bad things with magic, and Hagrid is a half giant who can do some really cool magic (like giving Dudley a pig's tail!). As readers, we're learning about the wizarding world as Harry does. This helps make Harry a relatable protagonist, and it allows Rowling to "translate" what's being shown to the reader through Harry's eyes. Again, this is a great example of a story with a "shallow" learning curve, which is very appropriate for middle-grade readers.
- Have you heard of The Rule of Threes? The Rule of Threes is a writing principle wherein the storyteller presents something three times for greater effect (or retention) in the narrative. For example, Rowling mentions the word "Muggle" for the third time in this scene and we finally get a definition of what it means. Per Hagrid, a Muggle is "what we call non-magic folk like them" (the Dursleys). You can use The Rule of Threes in your own writing to create an effect like this, whether it be three progressive complications, three mentions of a detail, or whatever you want, really!

SCENE 6
DIAGON ALLEY
CHAPTER 5

6,557 words

"Harry woke early the next ... blinked and Hagrid had gone."

Summary: Harry and Hagrid travel to Diagon Alley to pick up school supplies and a package for Dumbledore. They pass through The Leaky Cauldron, where every wizard and witch (including his soon-to-be professor, Quirrell) recognizes Harry, and then they visit Gringotts where they retrieve Harry's money and a mysterious package for Dumbledore that Harry is *very* curious about. After that, Harry gets fitted for robes at Madam Malkin's, where he meets an unnamed first-year student he immediately dislikes, and then they visit their last stop, Ollivanders, where Harry purchases a wand. Mr. Ollivander has *a lot* to say about Harry's legacy—including that the world can expect great things from him, especially now that the brother of Voldemort's wand chose him. Later, Harry tells Hagrid that he doesn't think he can live up to everyone's expectations of him, but Hagrid reassures Harry that everything will be fine once he gets to Hogwarts.

ANALYZING THE SCENE

STORY EVENT

A Story Event is an active change of a universal human value for one or more characters as a result of conflict (one character's desires clash with another's, or an environmental shift changes the value positively or negatively).

A Working Scene contains at least one Story Event. To determine a scene's Story Event, answer these four Socratic questions:

1. What are the characters literally doing—that is, what are their micro on-the-surface actions? Reader's Perspective (OTS)

Harry and Hagrid shop for school supplies in Diagon Alley.
OTS Change (Harry): Muggle World to Wizarding World / Traveling to Shopping

2. What is the essential tactic of the characters—that is, what above-the-surface macro behaviors are they employing that are linked to a universal human value? Character's Perspective (ATS)

Harry wants to understand this new world that he's now a part of, but once he gets to Diagon Alley, he realizes there's so much he doesn't know and he starts feeling insecure. The wizarding world wants to welcome Harry back with open arms and give him the recognition he deserves, but this makes Harry uncomfortable. He doesn't know if he has what it takes to live up to other people's expectations.
ATS Change (Harry): Ignorance to Knowledge / Awe to Insecurity

3. What beyond-the-surface universal human values have changed for one or more characters in the scene? Which one of those value changes is most important and should be included in the Story Grid Spreadsheet? Author's Perspective (BTS)

Although Harry feels insecure about his ability to assimilate into the wizarding world (and to live up to his reputation), he succeeds in collecting everything he needs to go to Hogwarts, learn all the necessary spells, forge the all-important alliances, and develop the confidence and courage needed to face Voldemort in the end. His visit to Gringotts is especially important because it piques Harry's curiosity about what's in the mysterious package. If Harry's not curious about this, he won't feel called to investigate it or protect it once he realizes it's at Hogwarts. And if he doesn't do this, Voldemort will succeed in coming to power again.

BTS Change (Harry): *Unequipped to Equipped*

4. The Scene Event Synthesis: What Story Event sums up the scene's on-the-surface, above-the-surface, and beyond-the-surface change? We will enter that event in the Story Grid Spreadsheet.

Harry and Hagrid visit Diagon Alley to purchase school supplies, and Harry grows more insecure about his place in the wizarding world, especially after visiting Ollivanders.

HOW THE SCENE ABIDES BY THE FIVE COMMANDMENTS OF STORYTELLING

Inciting Incident: Causal. The witches and wizards in the Leaky Cauldron all recognize Harry and welcome him back into the wizarding world.

Turning Point Progressive Complication: Active. Mr. Ollivander says the world can expect great things from Harry.

Crisis: Best Bad Choice. Will Harry go through with his decision to go to Hogwarts and risk disappointing himself and the rest of the wizarding world? Or will he let his fears and insecurities win and end up back in his miserable life at the Dursleys?

Climax: Harry shares his fears with Hagrid and decides to move forward with his plans.

Resolution: Harry feels nervous (but ready) to go to Hogwarts. He gets on a train and heads back to the Dursleys for the rest of the summer.

NOTES

- This scene is a great example of a set-piece action sequence that's not very "high stakes" feeling, but is still very satisfying for the reader. Remember: A set-piece action sequence is a scene (or group of scenes) that move the story forward in a *significant* way, and they're often the larger, more memorable moments that your external plot and your character's internal arc pivot around. So, yes, this scene *does* span multiple locations and include a few significant character interactions, but the directive of the scene is so strong that it works. That being said, throughout our analysis of the entire *Harry Potter* series, we see that Rowling shifts to a more traditional definition of writing "in scenes" (and combines multiple scenes to create a set-piece action sequence versus creating a set-piece action sequence out of one scene) as she develops her skillset and the target age range shifts to Young Adult, allowing for an expanded word count.
- Notice that The Leaky Cauldron is hidden from Muggles much like 12 Grimmauld Place is hidden in book five, *Harry Potter and the Order of the Phoenix*. This early setup of places being hidden from Muggles makes the existence of 12 Grimmauld Place more believable once we get to book five.
- Remember how McGonagall mentioned Dedalus in chapter one? And then we hear about the tiny man in a top hat who bowed to Harry on the street in chapter two? Harry finally meets him in the Leaky Cauldron! This is a fun payoff for readers that (again) abides by The Rule of Threes. But it's not the last time we see Dedalus Diggle. In book seven, *Harry Potter and the Deathly Hallows,* he'll be part of the guard that escorts the Dursleys away from Privet Drive. It's fun to notice how Rowling makes later use

of characters even with small roles. You can do this when writing a series too!
- Rowling introduces Professor Quirrell (who is not yet wearing a turban!) in this scene. He has a nervous demeanor, so it's easy for readers to dismiss him as a passive "throw-away" type of character versus someone significant enough to cause so much trouble. Quirrell's presence in Diagon Alley is a big clue that readers easily dismiss because so much is going on, and Quirrell seems like such an unlikely thief.
- This is the first time we hear about Bathilda Bagshot, the author of one of Harry's schoolbooks (*A History of Magic*). This setup is paid off throughout the series every time Hermione references the text for information or guidance. In a way, it's almost as if this text book (and Hermione's *collection* of textbooks) serve the same role as a mentor figure. You can get creative with conventional characters like this in your story, too.
- Notice how Rowling highlighted the details that made Gringotts feel dangerous to Harry and the reader. The poem on the front door hints that something dangerous lives inside the bank, hundreds of goblins are present (including Griphook, who becomes an important character in book seven), and Harry even thinks he sees a dragon living within the vaults. Later on when we learn that someone *did* try to rob Gringotts, these details make us wonder things like: What kind of person would try to rob Gringotts if it's so dangerous? What were they after, and why?
- Harry hears someone mention the new Nimbus 2000 broom. This setup is paid off in chapter nine, "The Midnight Duel," where Harry gets this exact same broom.
- Malfoy mentions Quidditch and how his "father says it's a crime if I'm not picked to play for my house" despite the fact that first-years hardly ever make the house teams. Not only does this give us great insight into Malfoy's character (he thinks he plays by different rules than everyone else and is *better* than everyone else, too), but it also makes sense why he's *so* mad when Harry makes the Quidditch team in chapter eight, "The Potions

Master." Also, in this scene alone, Malfoy shows his prejudice against Hufflepuffs, then against Hagrid, and finally against Muggles. This behavior will continue throughout the story.
- Hagrid mentions the rule that students can't use magic in the Muggle world except for in very special circumstances. This puts boundaries on the magic system Rowling created, which helps in terms of believability. In other words, magic can't do or solve everything if kids aren't allowed to use it outside of school. But also, in the final chapter, Hagrid reminds Harry that Dudley doesn't know Harry can't use magic outside school, which adds a bit of humor to the otherwise gloomy fact that Harry has to return to the Dursleys for the summer.
- Hagrid tells Harry that toads (as student companions) went out of fashion years ago. This sets up just one of the reasons why Neville gets bullied by the Slytherins. He has an out-of-fashion pet toad named Trevor.
- Ollivander tells Harry: "It's the wand that chooses the wizard," and, "You'll never get such good results with another wizard's wand." This implies (and "shows" rather than "tells) that wands are sentient. Ollivander also reveals that not only did he sell Voldemort the wand that gave Harry his lightning bolt shaped scar, but also that both wands contain a feather from the same phoenix. We don't know what this means yet, but we don't have to! These details are enough to evoke fear in readers (and in Harry) about a possible confrontation with Voldemort in the future. Also, Ollivander recognizes Harry because he has his mother's eyes, which echoes what Hagrid said in chapter four, "The Keeper of the Keys." Clearly, this detail is going to be important, but we don't understand why just yet.
- In this scene, did you notice how Rowling goes all out with the world-building details but doesn't go too deep into anything that isn't relevant to what Harry's doing in the scene? We don't learn about things like the Sorting Hat or the Great Hall because they don't matter yet. We only briefly hear about Quidditch and the school houses during Harry's interaction with Malfoy, but just enough to pique our interest of what's coming. Many first-time

writers go nuts with world-building details, or they intentionally draw the reader's attention to something, making it overly obvious or unnecessarily distracting from what's happening in the scene. Rowling's delivery of these important details is far more casual. She lets us encounter the world as Harry does since, like us, he's seeing it for the first time—and this is especially appropriate for middle-grade readers, who need a little bit more time and space to soak everything in.

- This scene is the Climax of the Beginning Hook. Although Harry has already decided to go to Hogwarts in the last chapter, his confidence in his decision wavers as he starts to realize how much he *doesn't* know about the wizarding world. However, Harry is nothing if not courageous, and by the end of this scene, he's still willing to commit to the future that awaits him at Hogwarts.

Even though Harry committing to the future is the most important part of this scene, that still leaves questions around the smaller moments *within* the scene that are arguably significant.

Let's take a look at how they each move the scene forward and why they're not necessarily scenes on their own.

1. The first part of the scene establishes Harry's scene goal—to purchase his school supplies in Diagon Alley. As Harry and Hagrid travel from the shack to London, we learn some important world-building information such as the *Daily Prophet* is the primary news source for witches and wizards, a Ministry of Magic governs the wizarding world, dragons exist and guard Gringotts, which makes it dangerous to try and rob, and Hagrid really wants a dragon! Although you *could* infer that Harry wants to keep asking Hagrid questions (but chooses not to because he's reading the newspaper), there's not a real crisis here.
2. Next, Harry and Hagrid pass through the Leaky Cauldron where every witch and wizard present (including Professor Quirrell) recognizes Harry and welcomes him back into the wizarding

world. Harry does not face a crisis here, but the internal conflict escalates. He's already a little nervous and unsure about his place in the wizarding world, but this is the first time he comes face to face with strangers who recognize him and have expectations of him based on a night he can't even remember.

3. Once they pass through the wall into Diagon Alley, Harry and Hagrid visit Gringotts, withdraw Harry's money, and retrieve a mysterious package for Dumbledore. Although Harry's curious about the package, he doesn't face a crisis here and his scene goal remains the same—to collect school supplies.

4. In Madam Malkin's robe shop, Harry meets an unnamed character (Draco Malfoy) who he instantly dislikes. Harry *does* face a crisis here (stand up for Hagrid or let Malfoy insult him), but it's not a big enough crisis to create a value shift in the scene. This interaction is more about establishing tension between Harry and Draco that will become the foundation for their conflict in this book and in the rest of the series. It's also a great example of Harry choosing good (Hagrid) versus evil (Malfoy). Because of that, this moment acts as a setup of Harry's character that pays off over and over again throughout the series. For example, in chapter nine, "The Midnight Duel," we'll see Harry choose to side with Neville (the victim in the scene, and the force of "good") over Malfoy (the antagonist in the scene, and the force of "evil").

5. After that, Harry and Hagrid gather all the remaining school supplies at Flourish and Blotts, the Apothecary, and Eeylops Owl Emporium. Harry (and the reader) learn important world-building information about the school rules and houses, including that Voldemort was in Slytherin, and that (according to Hagrid) "there's not a single witch or wizard who went bad who wasn't in Slytherin." This further associates Malfoy with evil because he said he's hoping to be in Slytherin, and it's the basis of why Harry asks the Sorting Hat to put him in Gryffindor in chapter seven, "The Sorting Hat." There's no crisis here and Harry's goal remains the same—to gather all of his school supplies. However, the internal conflict

Harry feels regarding his place in the wizarding world continues to build.

6. Then, Harry and Hagrid visit Ollivanders to get a wand. Harry does not face a crisis while in Ollivanders, but it's clear he's feeling even more insecure after his interaction with Mr. Ollivander, and after he gets his wand. Because of this, Harry faces the scene crisis. Should he *really* go to Hogwarts? Is venturing into the unknown worth the risk? What if he's unable to live up to his reputation and other people's expectations of him?

7. Finally, Harry and Hagrid leave Diagon Alley and share a meal. Harry expresses his concerns about reentering the wizarding world, saying, "Everyone thinks I'm special… but I don't know anything about magic at all. How can they expect great things? I'm famous and I can't even remember what I'm famous for." He expresses the feelings that have been building throughout the entire scene but ultimately decides to move forward with his plan to go to Hogwarts.

So, as you can see, each smaller moment within this scene helps Harry accomplish his scene goal (to purchase school supplies) yet puts pressure on his internal obstacle at the same time. If it helps you to plan out your story in terms of smaller moments (for example, if you were writing a scene like Diagon Alley, and it's more helpful to think of each different interaction as a "scene"), you can definitely plan your story this way! However, during revisions, you might find that you have multiple "scenes" in a row with the same (or too similar of a) value shift. When this happens, consider whether you can merge those smaller moments into one scene (with your character pursuing one goal) by turning those smaller moments into progressive complications within that scene. Obviously, this is not going to be the solution in every single scenario, but it's nice to know you have options that aren't "kill your darlings"!

SCENE 7

THE JOURNEY FROM PLATFORM NINE AND THREE-QUARTERS

CHAPTER 6

2,488 words

"Harry's last month with the ... what he was leaving behind"

Summary: Harry spends the last month of summer at the Dursleys' anxiously awaiting the start of term. However, when September first arrives, Harry has trouble navigating his way through Platform Nine and Three-Quarters on his own. Luckily, Harry overhears a family of redheads say something about "Muggles," and he enlists their help getting through the platform and onto the Hogwarts Express.

ANALYZING THE SCENE

STORY EVENT

A Story Event is an active change of a universal human value for one or more characters as a result of conflict (one character's desires clash with another's, or an environmental shift changes the value positively or negatively).

A Working Scene contains at least one Story Event. To determine a scene's Story Event, answer these four Socratic questions:

1. **What are the characters literally doing—that is, what are their micro on-the-surface actions? Reader's Perspective (OTS)**

> Harry goes to King's Cross Station and boards the Hogwarts Express.
> OTS Change (Harry): Muggle World to Wizarding World

2. **What is the essential tactic of the characters—that is, what above-the-surface macro behaviors are they employing that are linked to a universal human value? Character's Perspective (ATS)**

> Harry wants to get onto Platform Nine and Three-Quarters so he can board the Hogwarts Express and attend Hogwarts, but this proves difficult when he doesn't have a guide and doesn't understand the magical world.
> ATS Change (Harry): Ignorance to Knowledge

3. **What beyond-the-surface universal human values have changed for one or more characters in the scene? Which one of those value changes is most important and should be included in the Story Grid Spreadsheet? Author's Perspective (BTS)**

> Although Harry leaves the safety and protection of his "normal world," it's critical that Harry goes to Hogwarts where he will gain the confidence and skills needed to face Voldemort and protect the Sorcerer's Stone. This is also Harry's first introduction to the Weasley family, and his relationship with them (especially Ron) will be paramount in his ability to survive.
> BTS Change (Harry): *Abandoned to Supported*

4. **The Scene Event Synthesis: What Story Event sums up the scene's on-the-surface, above-the-surface, and beyond-the-surface change? We will enter that event in the Story Grid Spreadsheet.**

> *Harry leaves the muggle world when he steps through Platform Nine and Three-Quarters and boards the Hogwarts Express.*

HOW THE SCENE ABIDES BY THE FIVE COMMANDMENTS OF STORYTELLING

Inciting Incident: Coincidental. Harry can't find platform nine and three-quarters.

Turning Point Progressive Complication: Revelation. Harry overhears a family (the Weasleys) talking about "Muggles."

Crisis: Best Bad Choice. Should Harry approach the family and ask for help getting onto the platform? Or should he try to find another way through and risk missing the train to Hogwarts?

Climax: Harry approaches the family and asks for help.

Resolution: With the help of the Weasley family, Harry steps through Platform Nine and Three-Quarters and boards the Hogwarts Express.

NOTES

- This scene is the Resolution of the Beginning Hook. By boarding the Hogwarts Express, Harry has officially left the "normal world" of the Beginning Hook and is entering the "unfamiliar world" of the Middle Buildup. There's no going back now!
- Harry's goal in this scene is to board the Hogwarts Express on time so that he can go to Hogwarts. To accomplish this goal, Harry first rides to the train station with Mr. Dursley, who points out that Platform Nine and Three-Quarters doesn't exist. This kicks off the conflict, which deepens when Harry can't find the platform. Then, he faces the scene crisis: Should he ask for help or miss the train? Because the goal doesn't change from start to finish, it makes sense to analyze this as one scene with escalating conflict versus multiple scenes with the same (or too similar of a) value shift.

- Unbeknownst to Harry, the Weasleys will become more of a family to him than the Dursleys ever were. This scene shows us the first of many times that Mrs. Weasley will act to support and protect Harry, like a mother would.
- We also get to see some of the classic archetypal character roles in this scene too. Character archetypes are types of characters that appear again and again in stories from cultures around the world and symbolize something universal in the human experience. For example, Fred and George Weasley are the tricksters, Ron is the sidekick and one of the guides in this new world, Ginny later becomes the love interest in book six, *Harry Potter and the Half-Blood Prince*, and Mrs. Weasley is a mother and mentor figure. You can draw on these universal archetypes when crafting your own stories to make your cast of characters more relatable to readers.
- This is the first time we see Percy Weasley and how unlike the rest of the Weasley family he is. This setup will pay off in book five, *Harry Potter and the Order of the Phoenix*, when Percy defects from the rest of his family and supports the Ministry of Magic instead. Although we can't say for sure how much Rowling knew about Percy's future role in the series while writing book one, it's fun to notice how, even here, Percy is the black sheep of the family. When crafting your own book series, consider how you can use characters that already exist to create these kinds of connections from book to book.
- Rowling mentions Neville and Lee Jordan here, but they don't become friends with Harry until later chapters. This is a great example of tight plotting because Rowling could have introduced Harry (and readers) to many other characters, but she chose two that will be significant later on. She uses Neville, specifically, to help highlight what it looks like (and what it means) to have courage. Again, this is probably something she sharpened through the editing process, so don't worry about having things like this figured out when writing your first (or even second) draft.

SCENE 8

THE JOURNEY FROM PLATFORM NINE AND THREE-QUARTERS

CHAPTER 6

3,783 words

"The door of the compartment ... times on the castle door."

Summary: Harry shares a train compartment with Ron Weasley and they get to know each other as the train travels to Hogwarts. Ron explains some of the nuances of the wizarding world including things like Chocolate Frogs and the school houses. Later, Harry meets Hermione and Neville, then Malfoy, Crabbe, and Goyle. When Malfoy extends a hand of friendship to Harry, Harry declines. Malfoy gets upset and threatens Harry, saying that if he's not careful, he'll go the same way as his (Harry's) parents. Shortly after, the train arrives at Hogwarts.

ANALYZING THE SCENE

STORY EVENT

A Story Event is an active change of a universal human value for one or more characters as a result of conflict (one character's desires clash with

another's, or an environmental shift changes the value positively or negatively).

A Working Scene contains at least one Story Event. To determine a scene's Story Event, answer these four Socratic questions:

1. **What are the characters literally doing—that is, what are their micro on-the-surface actions? Reader's Perspective (OTS)**

Harry rides the train to Hogwarts and gets to know some of his fellow students.
OTS Change (Harry): King's Cross Station to Hogwarts / Traveling to Arriving

2. **What is the essential tactic of the characters—that is, what above-the-surface macro behaviors are they employing that are linked to a universal human value? Character's Perspective (ATS)**

Harry wants to get to know Ron Weasley, and Ron wants to get to know Harry, too. Draco Malfoy wants to meet Harry Potter and get him on his "side," but Harry's not interested. Once the train arrives at Hogwarts, all the excitement Harry felt while getting to know Ron turns to nerves.
ATS Change (Harry): Excited to Nervous / Alone to Making Friends (and Enemies)

3. **What beyond-the-surface universal human values have changed for one or more characters in the scene? Which one of those value changes is most important and should be included in the Story Grid Spreadsheet? Author's Perspective (BTS)**

Harry gains his main friend and ally, Ron Weasley, who will be instrumental in not only his knowledge of the wizarding world and how to function in it but who will also ground and support Harry in his humble nature. This friendship *aids* Harry's ability to survive. But by defending his friendship with Ron, Harry also solidifies his primary day-to-day antagonist, Draco Malfoy—and this rivalry *harms* Harry's ability to survive.
BTS Change (Harry): *Alone to Making Friends (and Enemies)*

4. **The Scene Event Synthesis:** What Story Event sums up the scene's on-the-surface, above-the-surface, and beyond-the-surface change? We will enter that event in the Story Grid Spreadsheet.

Harry makes friends with Ron while on the Hogwarts Express and later defends this friendship with Ron against Draco Malfoy.

HOW THE SCENE ABIDES BY THE FIVE COMMANDMENTS OF STORYTELLING

Inciting Incident: Coincidental. Harry meets Ron Weasley.

Turning Point Progressive Complication: Active. Malfoy insults Ron and extends an offer of friendship to Harry.

Crisis: Best Bad Choice. Should Harry accept Malfoy's offer of friendship and risk alienating Ron? Or should he decline Malfoy's offer and risk having an enemy instead?

Climax: Harry refuses to shake Malfoy's hand, thus declining his offer of friendship.

Resolution: Harry and Ron become friends, and the train arrives at Hogwarts.

NOTES

- Although this scene includes a few different significant character interactions, I analyzed it as one scene for two reasons —1) Harry is pursuing one overarching goal: to get to Hogwarts, and 2) all of his interactions add up to one major value shift: He ends the scene having made both friends and enemies. When planning and writing your own stories, feel free to break up moments (or conversations) like this as if they were each one "scene" with their own set of Five Commandments. You can always re-evaluate once you get to the editing stage. For example, Harry *does* face a small crisis around whether to share his pastries, cakes, and candies with Ron (or not), and this *does* contribute to the two of them becoming friends. But if you zoom out and look at the bigger picture, Harry's decision to defend his friendship with Ron creates the same kind of value shift (strangers to friends) *while also* establishing Malfoy as Harry's day-to-day antagonist. In other words, it's the same value shift, but it's more significant here because it's nestled within another. Also, it's worth pointing out that if you *did* analyze this as two separate scenes, it would bring you to the same conclusion, so there's no "wrong" answer!

- For the first time ever, Harry has a sense of agency. He can sit where he wants, talk to who he wants, eat whatever he wants, and ask all the questions that pop into his mind. Although we've felt a sense of wonder in the previous two scenes, that feeling increases in this scene because Harry's experiencing things on his own versus with an adult present. The imposter syndrome Harry feels is still present, but we can see that it's alleviated when he's in the company of friends (Ron).
- Rowling gives us another glimpse into Harry's character in this scene. First, we see Harry's humility through his conversation with Ron. Later, we see his courage and loyalty when he stands up to Malfoy. This is also the first time he's had to deal with his fame and answer questions about his past on his own. His modesty reflects his character. He's never wanted fame and he'll never revel in it like others might.
- Rowling introduces us to all kinds of candies and treats that are specific to Harry's world. But notice how she's only dolling out world-building details that are relevant to what's happening in the scene versus including everything she knows. This strategy helps the details she includes feel like an organic part of the scene rather than an info-dump that pulls readers out of the scene.

- Note that Harry doesn't just buy a bar of chocolate off the snack cart. He buys a chocolate frog that reveals the name of a person (Dumbledore) who holds a key plot clue (Nicolas Flamel's connection to the Sorcerer's Stone). Harry, Ron and Hermione spend a ton of time trying to figure out who Flamel is later in the story, but the information is already there for Harry and the reader. Being that it's such a small detail, and not the focal point of the scene, it's easy for the reader (and Harry) to overlook this clue and dismiss it as not important or just part of the background. Most of Rowling's world-building details add something "extra," like hiding or highlighting a clue or providing history or backstory of the characters and the setting. Few of her world-building details or world-building elements are thrown in as fluff, which just proves Rowling's a master of her craft.
- Harry meets Neville Longbottom and Hermione Granger, who will later become his friends. Hermione establishes herself as a know-it-all—something that first annoys Harry and Ron but comes in handy throughout the book and the series.
- Scabbers makes his first appearance in this scene, and he'll play an important role as Voldemort's primary sidekick later in the series. The spell Ron is trying to do to turn Scabbers yellow (setup) doesn't work because Scabbers is not a rat, he's an Animagus, a witch or wizard who can turn into an animal. We only learn the truth about this moment (payoff) in book three, *Harry Potter and the Prisoner of Azkaban*. Scabbers defends Ron and Harry by biting Goyle's hand—another clue that he's not just a common rat. That being said, we can only guess how much Rowling knew about Scabbers's future role in the series while writing book one. Ron is a first-year student who isn't *that* great at doing magic. This alone is a good enough reason for readers to believe that Ron's at fault for the spell not working. Later, it's something Rowling could turn into a clue if it wasn't something she had originally planned on using as a clue. You can do the same thing with the details in your series, so don't panic if you don't have all the

connections figured out while outlining or writing the first book or two.
- Ron tells Harry that his brother, Charlie, is in Romania studying dragons. This setup pays off later in the book when Harry helps Hagrid get rid of Norbert in chapter fourteen, "Norbert the Norweigan Ridgeback." If Rowling didn't set this detail up and then echo it a few times in later scenes, it would feel like a "too convenient" solution later on.
- Ron tells Harry that his other brother, Bill, works at Gringotts. This conversation reminds Ron about an article in the paper where somebody was robbing a high security vault at Gringotts. Harry finds this interesting, but Ron quickly changes the subject and starts talking about Quidditch. This small mention of Gringotts gives Harry (and the reader) a clue about what happened that day in Diagon Alley, but Harry (and the reader) dismiss it because Ron's so excited about Quidditch. This is a great (and organic) way to remind the reader (and Harry) about the package Hagrid retrieved from Gringotts and to pique Harry's forward-moving curiosity about what *really* happened that day in Diagon Alley.
- Malfoy shows his prejudiced ways *again* when he tries to convince Harry to ditch Ron and sit with the soon-to-be Slytherins instead. Ron confirms Malfoy's family were on Voldemort's side before he disappeared, and Harry feels another prickle of fear when Voldemort's name is mentioned. This is another great example of how Harry is capable of telling good from bad and how he makes decisions based on his gut feelings. We also get a glimpse at Malfoy's family's allegiance when he threatens Harry, saying that if he's not careful, he'll go the same way as his (Harry's) parents.
- Notice that the other students who come into Harry and Ron's compartment act as complications to Harry's scene goal. He wants to get to know Ron, but then Hermione and Neville interrupt, followed by Malfoy, Crabbe and Goyle. When crafting your own scenes, it's important to know your point of view

character's goals and expectations because this helps you put the conflict into context.

SCENE 9

THE SORTING HAT

CHAPTER 7

4,464 words

"The door swung open at ... remember the dream at all."

Summary: Once inside the castle, Professor McGonagall informs the students that they must be sorted into one of the four school houses—Gryffindor, Hufflepuff, Ravenclaw, or Slytherin—before dinner. Harry asks the Sorting Hat to place him in any house but Slytherin and gets his wish when it sorts him into Gryffindor. Shortly after joining the rest of the Gryffindors at their table, Harry makes eye contact with a black-haired, hooked-nose teacher, and his scar lights up in pain. Later that night he has nightmares about the night his parents died, Professor Quirrell's turban, being transferred to Slytherin, and being laughed at by Snape and Malfoy.

ANALYZING THE SCENE

STORY EVENT

A Story Event is an active change of a universal human value for one or more characters as a result of conflict (one character's desires clash with another's, or an environmental shift changes the value positively or negatively).

A Working Scene contains at least one Story Event. To determine a scene's Story Event, answer these four Socratic questions:

1. What are the characters literally doing—that is, what are their micro on-the-surface actions? Reader's Perspective (OTS)

Harry and the other first-year students enter the castle and get sorted into their school houses.
OTS Change (Harry): Outside to Inside / First-Years to Specific Houses

2. What is the essential tactic of the characters—that is, what above-the-surface macro behaviors are they employing that are linked to a universal human value? Character's Perspective (ATS)

Harry wants to get settled and find out where he belongs at Hogwarts, but when the Sorting Hat considers putting him in Slytherin, he panics. Harry's values don't align with what he's seen and heard about Slytherin so far, but the Sorting Hat believes he'd do well in Slytherin.
ATS Change (Harry): Nervous to Relieved

3. What beyond-the-surface universal human values have changed for one or more characters in the scene? Which one of those value changes is most important and should be included in the Story Grid Spreadsheet? Author's Perspective (BTS)

Although finally safe at Hogwarts and sorted into a worthy house, Harry is now in close proximity to Professor Quirrell (danger) and the Sorcerer's Stone. However, being sorted into Gryffindor (rather than

Slytherin) gives Harry the best chance to develop his core strengths—his humility, courage, and loyalty (since these are Gryffindor's values).

BTS Change (Harry): *Potential for Danger to Potential for Growth*

4. The Scene Event Synthesis: What Story Event sums up the scene's on-the-surface, above-the-surface, and beyond-the-surface change? We will enter that event in the Story Grid Spreadsheet.

Harry is sorted into Gryffindor after pleading with the Sorting Hat to not put him in Slytherin.

HOW THE SCENE ABIDES BY THE FIVE COMMANDMENTS OF STORYTELLING

Inciting Incident: Causal. Professor McGonagall tells the first-year students they will be sorted into their school houses before dinner.

Turning Point Progressive Complication: Active. The Sorting Hat seems to have trouble choosing where to put Harry and mentions he'd do well in Slytherin.

Crisis: Best Bad Choice. Should Harry speak up about not wanting to be in Slytherin? Or should he let the Sorting Hat choose and risk being sorted into Slytherin?

Climax: Harry tells the Sorting Hat he doesn't want to be in Slytherin.

Resolution: Harry feels relieved when he's sorted into Gryffindor with Ron. He meets the rest of his house, eats a delicious meal, and listens to Dumbledor's start-of-term speech. However, later that night he has nightmares about the night his parents died, Professor Quirrell's turban, being transferred to Slytherin, and being laughed at by Snape and Malfoy.

NOTES

- This is the Inciting Incident of the Middle Buildup. Exiting this scene, Harry suspects that Snape dislikes him, but he can't fathom why. He thinks making eye contact with Snape caused his scar to light up in pain, and because of this, readers (and Harry) are led to believe Snape's a bad guy. In other words, Rowling has effectively set up Snape as a red herring, masking the truth about Quirrell. And speaking of Quirrell, did you notice that he's sitting *right next to* Snape when Harry makes eye contact with him? This is how Rowling hides the truth from the reader while also planting true clues in the same scene. Also, this is the first time we see Quirrell wearing a turban. Voldemort is officially at Hogwarts!
- McGonagall appears to have the authority of a stereotypically strict teacher. This familiar archetypal role helps ground readers in the magical world and also provides a nice counterbalance to Hagrid's less than "formal" personality. Plus, it's a role many middle-grade readers can relate to, which draws them into the story even more.
- When Professor McGonagall says, "Your house will be something like your family within Hogwarts," Harry starts to worry what will happen if he's not picked for any house. His imposter syndrome has kicked in again—and rightly so! He's been so conditioned to believe that he doesn't belong (with the Dursleys) that this is a realistic and believable worry for him. This is also why we root for him and hope he *does* find that sense of family and belonging here at Hogwarts.
- The Hogwarts ghosts make an appearance for the first time. Harry overhears the ghosts arguing about Peeves's antics in this scene, which is a setup for Peeves being a troublemaker/trickster throughout this book (and the series). Later, when the students encounter Peeves on the way to Gryffindor Tower, Percy threatens him by saying he'll tell the Bloody Baron what he's up to. Percy tells Harry that the Bloody Baron is the only one Peeves is afraid of, and Harry uses this to his advantage in chapter nine,

"The Midnight Duel," when he sneaks out of Gryffindor Tower to meet Malfoy for the Wizard's Duel.

- As a joke, Fred told Ron he'd have to wrestle a troll to be sorted into a house. The mention of a troll is a great setup for when Harry and Ron battle the troll in the girl's bathroom in chapter ten, "Halloween." This may seem like a throwaway detail, but it subconsciously lets readers know that we can expect to see a troll at some point in this book or series.

- Harry wishes they could be sorted in private because he doesn't want everyone's attention on him. This humility or desire to remain out of the spotlight is something we've seen in Harry since the beginning of the book—first, in chapter five when he goes to Diagon Alley for the first time, and then again in chapter six, "The Journey from Platform Nine and Three-Quarters," when his fellow students recognize him on the Hogwarts Express. Throughout the series, Harry eases into the spotlight as he learns to accept his role as "The Chosen One." This is one of the ways Rowling shows Harry's growth throughout the series, and it all starts here in book one.

- We get another great hint about Malfoy's character in this scene. He's such a bad seed that the Sorting Hat doesn't even need to touch his head before it sorts him into Slytherin. Remember what Hagrid said about Slytherin? In chapter five, "Diagon Alley," he says, "There's not a single witch or wizard who went bad who wasn't in Slytherin. You-Know-Who was one." This tells us everything we need to know about Malfoy's character, and it echoes the behavior we've already seen from him, too.

- Most of what we learn about the traits of the school houses are established in this scene. Hufflepuffs are loyal, Ravenclaws are wise, Slytherins are cunning, and Gryffindors are brave. The Sorting Hat thinks Harry would have done well in Slytherin because he *does* possess some Slytherin traits. But as we'll see in this book and throughout the series, most people display traits from *all* the houses. It's not a black and white sorting system. Harry will learn this important lesson throughout the series; however, in this first book, we do see how Harry's viewpoint of the houses—be it a bit black and white—defines his characteristics as a Gryffindor. More importantly, we see how these traits influence Harry's climatic decision in the end: He chooses *not* to follow in Voldemort's footsteps and instead defies him.

- Once sorted, Harry experiences a fresh start with his fellow first-years. This rite of passage is familiar to many middle-grade readers starting a new school. This allows middle-grade readers to empathize with Harry and share his joy and nervousness at being in a new (and unfamiliar) environment. It also grounds the reader in the "familiar" despite the story taking place in a magical world.

- We can only guess whether or not Rowling knew what happened to Neville's parents when writing book one, or if she developed their backstory later. But what we *can* learn from this scene is that it doesn't really matter! The only thing Harry (and the reader) learn about Neville in this scene is that he was raised by his grandmother. And that's enough! This shows us that, as writers, we don't *have to* have every little detail planned out for a series when writing book one—nor should we put our writing on hold until we develop all the details. Instead, trust the process and know that you can always dip back into characters or details in a later book to expand their backstories or functions.

- Although Dumbledore's introduced in a jovial (and kind of silly) manner, he delivers some really important warnings. First, the forest on the school grounds is forbidden to all students. This setup pays off later when Harry serves detention in the forest, and we learn why it's off limits and so dangerous for the students. Second, Dumbledore says the "third-floor corridor on the right-hand side is out of bounds to everyone who does not wish to die a very painful death." This setup pays off later when Harry, Ron, and Hermione realize a very dangerous three-headed dog lives there.

- Harry's nightmare is very purposeful. Quirrell's turban talks to Harry, telling him to transfer to Slytherin because it's his destiny.

Then Malfoy turns into Snape, who has a high and cold laugh, and Harry sees a burst of green light. Essentially, Harry's dream represents three levels of external antagonism that Harry has to face throughout the story: Malfoy, Snape and Quirrell/Voldemort. Malfoy is the most accessible source of antagonism given that he's the same age as Harry and will be attending some of the same classes. He's also necessary because it probably wouldn't have worked out so well to have all of Harry's conflict come from the adults in his life. Snape is the second most accessible source of antagonism because though he's always around, he's an adult and doesn't have the same level of day-to-day access to Harry that Malfoy does. Quirrell/Voldemort is the least accessible source of antagonism, partly because Voldemort isn't in his corporeal form yet and because Voldemort is the series antagonist. Notice that Harry must "defeat" or come to terms with each of these sources of antagonism in this order—from most accessible (Malfoy) to least accessible (Voldemort) both within this book and within the series. It's not a coincidence that Harry has this dream here right as the external action plot kicks off!

SCENE 10

THE POTIONS MASTER

CHAPTER 8

3,050 words

"*"There, look." "Where?" "Next ... didn't want to tell Harry?"*

Summary: Harry attends his first week of classes, which go well until Potions where Professor Snape picks on him. After class, Harry and Ron go to Hagrid's house, where Harry recounts his experience with Snape, but Hagrid dismisses Harry's concerns, telling him not to worry. Harry sees a cutting from the *Daily Prophet* about the Gringotts robbery and he wonders if the package Hagrid retrieved from vault 713 could be what the thieves were after, but Hagrid won't share his opinion or any information on that either. Harry can't shake the feeling that Hagrid isn't telling the whole truth about Snape or the package, and he's determined to learn the truth.

ANALYZING THE SCENE

STORY EVENT

A Story Event is an active change of a universal human value for one or more characters as a result of conflict (one character's desires clash with another's, or an environmental shift changes the value positively or negatively).

A Working Scene contains at least one Story Event. To determine a scene's Story Event, answer these four Socratic questions:

1. What are the characters literally doing—that is, what are their micro on-the-surface actions? Reader's Perspective (OTS)

Harry, Ron, and Hermione attend Potions class, and later, Harry and Ron visit Hagrid.
OTS Change (Harry): Hogwarts Castle to Hagrid's Hut / Attending Class to Visiting Hagrid

2. What is the essential tactic of the characters—that is, what above-the-surface macro behaviors are they employing that are linked to a universal human value? Character's Perspective - ATS

Harry looks forward to his first week of classes but has trouble concentrating due to the effects of his reputation. By this point, everybody at Hogwarts is aware that Harry Potter is at school with them. He's a celebrity and this makes him very uncomfortable. Things get worse when Professor Snape picks on Harry to show everyone (including Harry) that he doesn't favor the "famous." Once inside Hagrid's house, Harry wants to know if Hagrid has any idea why Snape hates him so much or what happened at Gringotts the day they visited, but Hagrid doesn't want to share his thoughts on either subject.
ATS Change (Harry): Celebrity Status to Punished for Fame / Concerned to Curious

3. What beyond-the-surface universal human values have changed for

one or more characters in the scene? Which one of those value changes is most important and should be included in the Story Grid Spreadsheet? Author's Perspective (BTS)

Harry exits this scene believing Snape hates him. Because of this, it's easy for Harry (and readers) to see Snape as "the bad guy." Every time Harry leans into this incorrect interpretation of Snape, he's looking the wrong way and ignoring the clues that Quirrell is up to no good. This threatens his ability to stay safe and out of trouble. On the other hand, this scene also reignites Harry's curiosity about the package from vault 713. Without the reminder from the *Daily Prophet* article, Harry might not follow the clues that ultimately lead him to discover the Sorcerer's Stone and come face to face with Voldemort.

BTS Change (Harry): *Ignorance to Ignorance Masked as Knowledge*

4. The Scene Event Synthesis: What Story Event sums up the scene's on-the-surface, above-the-surface, and beyond-the-surface change? We will enter that event in the Story Grid Spreadsheet.

Snape bullies Harry during Potions class. Later Harry visits Hagrid and questions him about Gringotts and Snape's dislike of him, but Hagrid dismisses Harry's concerns.

HOW THE SCENE ABIDES BY THE FIVE COMMANDMENTS OF STORYTELLING

Inciting Incident: Causal. Ron mentions they have double Potions with the Slytherins today.

Turning Point Progressive Complication: Active. In Potions class, Snape accuses Harry of letting Neville make a mistake (not adding the porcupine quills before removing the cauldron from the fire) in order to make himself look good.

Crisis: Best Bad Choice. Should Harry stand up for himself and argue with

Snape's interpretation of events? Or should he keep quiet to avoid making things worse?

Climax: Harry stays quiet and doesn't stand up for himself.

Resolution: After Potions class, Harry and Ron visit with Hagrid. Harry tells Hagrid about Potions class and how Snape seems to hate him. Hagrid dismisses Harry's worries and says that Snape hardly likes anyone, so don't worry about it. Harry reads a *Daily Prophet* article about the Gringotts robbery and realizes it happened the same day that he and Hagrid were there. Harry is convinced that the thieves were after the package Hagrid took from vault 713 and that Hagrid is keeping something from Harry about why Professor Snape dislikes him.

NOTES

- Although this scene spans multiple locations and includes a few significant character interactions, I analyzed it as one scene for two reasons—1) Harry is pursuing one overarching goal—to survive his first week of classes (including the class he's been dreading, Potions with Professor Snape), and 2) everything adds up to one major development: Harry believes Snape hates him and is a bad guy. When planning and writing your own stories, feel free to break up moments like this as if they were each one "scene" with their own set of Five Commandments. You can always re-evaluate things once you get to the editing stage. For example, in Hagrid's hut, you could infer a crisis from both Harry and Hagrid's perspective. Harry wants more information about Snape and the Gringotts robbery, so you can imagine how Harry *might* feel like pushing Hagrid for more information after Hagrid dismisses Harry's concerns. You could also assume Hagrid faces a crisis about how much to tell Harry. Technically, Harry's right. Snape *does* dislike him, but not for any obvious reason and certainly not for any reason Hagrid can share.

However, neither of these crisis moments are on the page. If you zoom out to look at what the scene's *really* about, it's about three things—1) catching readers up with Harry's first week (we see this via narrative summary), 2) establishing the conflict and tension between Harry and Snape (which unfolds on the page in real-time), and 3) reigniting Harry's interest about the Gringotts robbery (which also unfolds in real-time). At the end of the scene, we're left with questions like: What *exactly* does Hagrid know about Snape? And more importantly, what does Hagrid know about the Gringotts break-in? Why won't he share what he knows with Harry? Again, we read on to find out the answers to these questions and more! So, all of this is to say that if you *did* analyze this chapter as two separate scenes, it would bring you to the same conclusion (more or less). There's no "wrong" answer!

- Although most middle-grade readers don't know what it's like to be a celebrity, they *do* know what it's like to experience the first week of a new school year. This helps ground the reader in a "familiar" situation and increases their empathy for Harry.
- Did you notice that this scene slightly changes pace from the previous scenes in Diagon Alley, on the Hogwarts Express, and during the Sorting Ceremony? Those chapters were full of wonder and excitement, but here we're brought back to the more mundane elements of Harry's life at Hogwarts. That being said, there's plenty of conflict within the mundane elements of Harry's new world, and this keeps readers engaged in the story.
- Rowling delivers a handful of new world-building details in this scene. We see staircases that move on their own, animated people in the portraits, doors that need to be tickled, and more. Because we learn this right alongside Harry (and because Rowling is judicious with which world-building details she includes), this allows readers to feel immersed in the story world without feeling overwhelmed.
- When Filch finds Harry and Ron trying to force their way through a door that leads to the third-floor corridor that is out of bounds, he threatens to lock them in the dungeons. Luckily,

Harry and Ron are rescued by Professor Quirrell who *just so happened* to be walking by. The fact that Quirrell is lurking around the third-floor corridor is a great setup that will pay off later when we find out the truth about what he's really up to.

- Rowling mentions that the Weasley twins know the secret passageways out of the school better than anyone. This setup will pay off later when Fred and George give Harry the Marauder's Map in book three, *Harry Potter and the Prisoner of Azkaban*. But consider why this works as a standalone detail versus a setup for a later book. Fred and George have already been introduced as tricksters. It makes total sense that they'd be privy to secret passageways underneath the school. Right? When writing your own series, don't stress over setups and payoffs that span multiple books, especially when writing the first draft. Instead, focus on making sure the details you include in book one *make sense for book one* and then see if you can use those details for another purpose later (if you want to).

- Some of the students say Quirrell's turban smells because it's full of garlic, "to ward off a vampire he'd met in Romania." This is a huge clue that J.K. Rowling masks behind a bit of fun and humor. On a second read, this makes us wonder if Quirrell was studying dragons in Romania to figure out how to get past the one guarding the vaults at Gringotts. Or was this where he got baby-Norbert to later offer Hagrid in exchange for information about how to get past Fluffy, the three-headed dog?

- Did you notice that some of the potions Snape mentions in class show up in later books? Powdered root of asphodel and wormwood make up a powerful sleeping potion called the Draught of the Living Dead. This comes back into play later in book six, *Harry Potter and the Half-Blood Prince*. Wolfsbane is a potion that relieves, but does not cure, the symptoms of lycanthropy. We see this again in book three, *Harry Potter and the Prisoner of Azkaban*. And finally, Snape mentions bezoars, which Harry uses to save Ron from poisoned mead in book six, *Harry Potter and the Half-Blood Prince*.

- This scene gives us proof that Snape favors Draco Malfoy over almost any other student. Because of this, we know Snape's future actions (and favoritism) are real and not something seen and felt through Harry's subjective perspective. This supports our belief in Harry as he pursues the truth about Snape and his connection to the package from vault 713. And it helps make Snape an effective red herring.
- This is the first time Harry and Ron visit Hagrid's hut, which is a place of comfort, safety, friendship, and privacy that Harry, Ron, and Hermione will visit often throughout the series. Because of that, this visit also offers a stark contrast and a little breather after Harry's horrible experience in Potions class.
- Mrs. Norris follows Hagrid every time he's in the school—possibly because Filch still thinks Hagrid is guilty of opening the Chamber of Secrets, which we find out in book two, *Harry Potter and the Chamber of Secrets*. However, if we pretend to know nothing about Hagrid's backstory, the fact that Filch is a strict rule enforcer is enough for us to understand his actions, even if we don't agree with them.
- Hagrid asks Ron how his brother, Charlie, is doing in Romania. We learned this in chapter six, "The Journey from Platform Nine and Three-Quarters". This is another reminder that Ron has a brother who knows about dragons. Without these reminders, Harry's idea to ask Charlie to help them relocate Hagrid's dragon, Norbert, might feel like too much of a coincidence.

SCENE 11
THE MIDNIGHT DUEL
CHAPTER 9

2,295 words

"Harry had never believed he ... an excellent Quidditch player himself."

Summary: During flying lessons with the Slytherins, Harry learns that he's a natural on a broom. Neville gets injured, leaving the Gryffindors and Slytherins alone to practice. Malfoy steals Neville's Remembrall and challenges Harry to come and get it. Despite Hermione's warnings, Harry goes after Malfoy and successfully retrieves the Remembrall but gets caught by Professor McGonagall. Harry worries he'll be expelled, but he's made Gryffindor Seeker instead.

ANALYZING THE SCENE

STORY EVENT

A Story Event is an active change of a universal human value for one or more characters as a result of conflict (one character's desires clash with

another's, or an environmental shift changes the value positively or negatively).

A Working Scene contains at least one Story Event. To determine a scene's Story Event, answer these four Socratic questions:

1. What are the characters literally doing—that is, what are their micro on-the-surface actions? Reader's Perspective (OTS)

Harry, the rest of the Gryffindor first-years, and the Slytherin first-years attend flying lessons with Madam Hooch.
OTS Change (Harry): Hogwarts Castle to Castle Grounds / Learning to Flying

2. What is the essential tactic of the characters—that is, what above-the-surface macro behaviors are they employing that are linked to a universal human value? Character's Perspective (ATS)

Harry wants to learn how to fly on a broom because he's been looking forward to learning to fly more than anything else at Hogwarts. But in doing so, he doesn't want to make a fool of himself in front of Malfoy. Malfoy wants to cause trouble and pick on Neville.
ATS Change (Harry): Nervous to Brave / Risk to Reward

3. What beyond-the-surface universal human values have changed for one or more characters in the scene? Which one of those value changes is most important and should be included in the Story Grid Spreadsheet? Author's Perspective (BTS)

Harry's confrontations with Malfoy present a major day-to-day antagonistic threat, which constantly threatens Harry's physical safety and enrollment at Hogwarts. This scene is the first of many where Malfoy will try to set Harry up for expulsion, and because Harry always stands up for his friends, he answers Malfoy's challenge. Luckily, Harry learns that he is an exceptional flier—a key skill that will come to Harry's aid not only in this book, when he faces one of the big obstacles protecting the Sorcerer's Stone, but also throughout the series as well.

BTS Change (Harry): *Threatened to Safe*

4. **The Scene Event Synthesis:** What Story Event sums up the scene's on-the-surface, above-the-surface, and beyond-the-surface change? We will enter that event in the Story Grid Spreadsheet.

Harry becomes the new Gryffindor Seeker after he stands up to Malfoy, and McGonagall sees Harry's exceptional flying skills.

HOW THE SCENE ABIDES BY THE FIVE COMMANDMENTS OF STORYTELLING

Inciting Incident: Causal. Harry learns that flying lessons start on Thursday—and that Gryffindor and Slytherin will learn together.

Turning Point Progressive Complication: Active. During flying lessons, Malfoy steals Neville's Remembrall and dares Harry to come get it.

Crisis: Best Bad Choice. Should Harry stand up to Malfoy and risk getting in trouble? Or should he keep quiet and let Malfoy get away with bullying Neville?

Climax: Harry mounts his broom and goes after Malfoy.

Resolution: Harry retrieves the Remembrall, and rather than expel him, McGonagall names Harry Gryffindor's Seeker.

NOTES

- Although this scene spans multiple locations and includes multiple significant character interactions, I analyzed it as one scene because everything contributes to one primary development: Harry learns how to fly and is made Gryffindor's

Seeker. The interactions within this scene primarily serve to escalate the tension between Malfoy and Harry and relieve some of it via the real-time conflict over Neville's Remembrall. If you look at the smaller moments (Neville getting a Remembrall in the Great Hall, learning how to fly, chasing Malfoy on broomstick, and talking to Oliver Wood), only one crisis moment is present. Should Harry stand up to Malfoy and risk getting in trouble? Or should he keep quiet and let Malfoy get away with bullying Neville? You could argue that McGonagall faces a crisis about what to do about Harry breaking the rules (punish him or make him Seeker), but it's not on the page. And really, this is just great storytelling! You *should* know what the other characters' goals, expectations, and decisions are in any given scene, even if they aren't on the page and obvious to the reader. That being said, if it's easier for you to break up the smaller moments like this as if they were each one "scene" with their own set of Five Commandments while planning and outlining your own story, go for it! You can always re-evaluate things once you get to the editing stage.

- Neville mentions that his Grandmother never let him ride a broomstick because he's accident-prone. This is a great setup for what's about to happen in the scene. It also speaks to Neville's overall character. He's clumsy!
- In this scene, we learn about a new magical item, the Remembrall—a small glass ball that tells you if you forgot to do something. We see the Remembrall come back again in book five, *Harry Potter and the Order of the Phoenix*.
- Hermione reads *Quidditch through the Ages* to prepare for the upcoming lesson (setup). In chapter eleven, "Quidditch," she lends Harry this very same book (payoff) once they've become friends. This is a smaller setup and payoff, but it's still fun to note. Even the smallest things Rowling mentions are significant in some way.
- Harry sticks up for Neville instead of joining in on the teasing with Malfoy. This is a great moment that reminds us of who Harry is. He's loyal to his friends and the other members of

Gryffindor house who are like his newfound family. Not only that, but moments like these give Harry the opportunity to become a hero. The more he answers these calls, the better wizard he becomes.

- Professor McGonagall tells Harry his father would have been proud of the fact that he's the new Gryffindor Seeker. We don't find out until much later that James Potter was a skilled Quidditch player, but a detail like this does more than inform Harry (and the reader) that McGonagall knew James and that he played Quidditch. It helps Harry feel a connection to his father that he's never felt before, and reinforces McGonagall's position on the side of "good."
- This is a great example of a surprising yet inevitable resolution to the scene. Harry fully expects to get in trouble, but instead, he's rewarded when McGonagall names him Seeker.

SCENE 12
THE MIDNIGHT DUEL
CHAPTER 9

2,603 words

"'You're joking!' It was dinnertime... seven hundred and thirteen was."

Summary: After Malfoy learns that Harry's the new Gryffindor Seeker, he challenges Harry to a wizard's duel at midnight. At half-past eleven, Harry and Ron leave the Gryffindor tower, and Hermione and Neville tag along. Malfoy doesn't show up for the duel, but Filch does! Harry, Ron, Hermione, and Neville run from Filch and end up coming face to face with a three-headed dog in the forbidden corridor on the third floor. Luckily, they escape, and once they're back in the dormitory, Harry realizes that the dog must be guarding something—the package from Gringotts!

ANALYZING THE SCENE

STORY EVENT

A Story Event is an active change of a universal human value for one or more characters as a result of conflict (one character's desires clash with

another's, or an environmental shift changes the value positively or negatively).

A Working Scene contains at least one Story Event. To determine a scene's Story Event, answer these four Socratic questions:

1. What are the characters literally doing—that is, what are their micro on-the-surface actions? Reader's Perspective (OTS)

Malfoy confronts Harry and Ron in the Great Hall, challenging them to a Wizard's Duel because he's upset that Harry was made Seeker. Later, when Malfoy doesn't show up for the duel, the kids must outrun Filch to get back to the Gryffindor common room.

OTS Change (Harry): Great Hall to Gryffindor Common Room to Unused Classroom

2. What is the essential tactic of the characters—that is, what above-the-surface macro behaviors are they employing that are linked to a universal human value? Character's Perspective (ATS)

Malfoy wants to get Harry in trouble, so he challenges Harry to a Wizard's Duel that he doesn't intend to attend. After Harry realizes Malfoy isn't coming, his goal shifts to evading Filch and Mrs. Norris so he doesn't get expelled. Filch wants to catch whoever's roaming around the forbidden third-floor corridor because he loves catching rule-breakers!

ATS Change (Harry): Risking Safety to Barely Escaping Danger

3. What beyond-the-surface universal human values have changed for one or more characters in the scene? Which one of those value changes is most important and should be included in the Story Grid Spreadsheet? Author's Perspective (BTS)

Although Harry is willing to put himself in immediate physical danger by meeting Malfoy for a Wizard's Duel, he did not anticipate coming face to face with a three-headed dog on the forbidden third floor. Luckily, he escapes unscathed. However, by encountering Fluffy, Harry realizes whatever Hagrid took from Gringotts is probably hidden underneath the trap door the dog is guarding. This makes Harry even more curious about what the package contains, and this curiosity puts Harry on the path toward danger (his confrontation with Voldemort) in the end.

BTS Change (Harry): *Ignorance to Knowledge*

4. The Scene Event Synthesis: What Story Event sums up the scene's on-the-surface, above-the-surface, and beyond-the-surface change? We will enter that event in the Story Grid Spreadsheet.

When Malfoy doesn't show up for the wizard's duel, Harry and friends accidentally discover that the three-headed dog in the forbidden corridor is probably guarding the package Hagrid retrieved from Gringotts.

HOW THE SCENE ABIDES BY THE FIVE COMMANDMENTS OF STORYTELLING

Inciting Incident: Causal. Malfoy challenges Harry to a duel in the trophy room at midnight.

Turning Point Progressive Complication: Action. Filch arrives in the trophy room and the kids realize Malfoy set them up.

Crisis: Best Bad Choice. Should they stay put and face their punishment, risking expulsion? Or should they run and try to make it back to Gryffindor tower but risk getting caught anyway?

Climax: The kids take their chances and run from Filch.

Resolution: Harry, Ron, Hermoine, and Neville end up in the forbidden third-floor corridor with a three-headed dog. Luckily, they make it back to the Gryffindor common room without getting caught. However, Harry is now convinced that the three-headed dog is guarding the package Hagrid took from Gringotts.

NOTES

- Notice how the stakes in this scene have been raised from the previous scene. In the last scene, Harry took an immediate physical risk by retrieving the Remembrall from Malfoy. He also risked getting expelled from Hogwarts by disobeying Madam Hooch's instructions. In this scene, the stakes are similar but a bit higher. Malfoy has challenged Harry to a duel, which could result in injury or actual death. They come across a dangerous three-headed dog, which could also result in injury or actual death. And if Filch catches them being in the "off-limits" corridor, they could still get expelled for disobeying rules. In other words, this scene deepens the stakes established in the last scene by layering in a new set of obstacles and challenges for Harry to face.
- This scene gives us a glimpse at Hermione's priorities when she says, "We could have all been killed—or worse, expelled." Throughout the story so far, we've been shown how different she is compared to Harry and Ron. However, her differences and her immense knowledge of spellwork save Harry and Ron on numerous occasions throughout this book and the series.
- Harry, Ron, and Hermione have to "defeat" three challenges in this scene: the first of many night-time encounters with Filch and Mrs. Norris, a run-in with Peeves the Poltergeist, and their first meeting with Fluffy, the three-headed dog. In all three scenarios, the kids flee the scene. This shows they haven't yet gained the courage, confidence, or skill to stand their ground, but there's potential. Hermione's intellect, Ron's courage, and Harry's instinct will grow and develop throughout the book and series and help them navigate the chamber under the school as well as stand up to Quirrell/Voldemort in the global climax.

SCENE 13
HALLOWEEN
CHAPTER 10

4,278 words

"Malfoy couldn't believe his eyes ... troll is one of them."

Summary: Harry receives a Nimbus 2000 broom in the mail, and later learns about Quidditch from Oliver Wood. Hermione is terribly upset that Harry was "rewarded" with a broom for breaking the rules, and their relationship becomes even more strained when Ron insults her during Charms class. Later, during dinner, Professor Quirrell announces that there's a troll in the dungeons, and the students panic. Dumbledore dismisses the students to the dormitories, but Harry realizes Hermione doesn't know about the troll, so they leave the group to go find her. On the way, Harry sees Snape headed in the opposite direction from everyone else (toward the third-floor corridor) but ultimately chooses not to follow him in favor of helping Hermione. Once they find Hermione, Harry and Ron battle the troll and knock it unconscious. The teachers arrive, Hermione takes the blame, and the three kids become friends.

ANALYZING THE SCENE

STORY EVENT

A Story Event is an active change of a universal human value for one or more characters as a result of conflict (one character's desires clash with another's, or an environmental shift changes the value positively or negatively).

A Working Scene contains at least one Story Event. To determine a scene's Story Event, answer these four Socratic questions:

1. **What are the characters literally doing—that is, what are their micro on-the-surface actions? Reader's Perspective (OTS)**

Harry learns the rules of Quidditch, attends Charms class, and (with Ron's help) saves Hermione from a troll.
OTS Change (Harry): Quidditch Pitch to Charms Class to Bathroom

2. **What is the essential tactic of the characters—that is, what above-the-surface macro behaviors are they employing that are linked to a universal human value? Character's Perspective (ATS)**

Professor Quirrell lets a troll into the castle, hoping the troll will provide enough of a distraction for him to go after the Sorcerer's Stone without being caught (also, bonus points if the troll kills Harry in the process). Harry and Ron want to save Hermione from the troll because, even though they're not "friends," they don't want Hermione to get hurt or worse, killed.
ATS Change (Harry): Not Friends to Friends / Divided to United

3. **What beyond-the-surface universal human values have changed for one or more characters in the scene? Which one of those value changes is most important and should be included in the Story Grid Spreadsheet? Author's Perspective (BTS)**

Harry and Ron risk their lives to save Hermione from the troll, and because of this, the three of them become friends. This friendship and the confidence Harry gains in this scene will be critical in terms of Harry's chances of survival when he faces Voldemort in the end.

BTS Change (Harry): In Danger to Safe

In Danger to Safe

4. The Scene Event Synthesis: What Story Event sums up the scene's on-the-surface, above-the-surface, and beyond-the-surface change? We will enter that event in the Story Grid Spreadsheet.

Harry and Ron save Hermione from the troll, and the three of them become friends.

HOW THE SCENE ABIDES BY THE FIVE COMMANDMENTS OF STORYTELLING

Inciting Incident: Causal. Professor Quirrell runs into the Great Hall yelling about a troll in the dungeons.

Turning Point Progressive Complication: Revelatory. After locking the troll in the girl's bathroom, Harry and Ron hear Hermione scream and realize they locked her in *with* the troll.

Crisis: Best Bad Choice. Should Harry and Ron go back to the girl's bathroom and try to rescue Hermione? Or should they go back to their dormitories and hope the teachers save Hermione?

Climax: Harry and Ron head back to the girl's bathroom.

Resolution: In an epic rescue, Harry and Ron take out the troll before it harms Hermione. Hermione takes the blame for their actions, and the three of them become friends.

NOTES

- This scene is the Turning Point of the Middle Buildup. Although this scene spans multiple locations and includes several important character interactions, there's only one meaningful value shift present. In the first part of the scene Harry receives an important object—his Nimbus 2000 broom. There's conflict when Malfoy realizes what Harry has, but it's diffused by Professor Flitwick and no real crisis is present. After that, Oliver Wood teaches Harry how to play Quidditch, but there's no crisis or value shift present here either. Only when Harry and Ron save Hermione from the troll do we see the actual scene-level value shift occur—and it's a big one. Harry, Ron, and Hermione have become friends! But not only that, things are *changing* here at Hogwarts. Someone let a troll into the school without regard for the students' lives. Even though readers don't realize what's *really* happening, Quirrell's stepping up his game.
- Professor Flitwick teaches the class "Wingardium Leviosa"— a spell to make objects fly. This is a great setup for the payoff at the end of the scene, where Ron uses the spell to save Hermione from the troll. In a way, this scene gives us a preview of how Ron and Hermione will challenge and support each other as their friendship and eventually romantic relationship develops throughout the series.
- Notice that Professor Quirrell and Professor Snape are in the same scene, allowing the reader to focus on Harry's suspicion of Snape, not Quirrell. Again, Snape is used as a red herring, distracting both Harry and the reader from the truth. In this scene, Harry and Ron see Snape heading toward the third floor instead of going to the dungeons with the other teachers. Harry thinks it's suspicious that Snape is moving in the opposite direction of everyone else, which causes Harry to suspect Professor Snape of trying to steal the Sorcerer's Stone. But later, we learn he was tracking Professor Quirrell, who was trying to figure out where the stone is and what's guarding it. Moments like this make the reveal at the end of the book so satisfying!

- Harry and Ron prove to Hermione that breaking the rules isn't always bad. If they had followed the rules and gone to their dormitory, Hermione might not have survived. This is important in terms of Hermione's growth over this book and the series as well as in terms of the kids becoming friends in this book.
- This scene escalates the conflict between Harry and Malfoy that's previously been established. We've seen Malfoy try to best Harry (and get him into trouble) over the past few scenes, but it finally feels like Harry's come out on top here. He's been given a new broom, Professor Flitwick backs him up when Malfoy tries to bully him, and he saves a fellow student from a troll. Perhaps things are finally starting to look up for Harry!
- Oliver Wood mentions that Charlie Weasley could have gone on to play professional Quidditch if he hadn't "gone off chasing dragons." We are reminded, again, of the connection between Charlie Weasley and dragons. It's a great way for Rowling to keep this future solution top of mind for Harry and readers.
- Notice how a pattern is starting to form in the crisis moments of each scene. Harry is often faced with a decision to either take matters into his own hands or to let the adults take care of the problems. Either way, he risks getting into trouble, getting injured, or even death in some cases. Over the course of the story, we will see Harry start to take matters into his own hands more and more as he gains confidence and skills. How a character behaves in these crisis moments over time is a great way to show readers their arc of internal change—especially if the crisis moments are similar in nature.

SCENE 14

QUIDDITCH

CHAPTER 11

932 words

"As they entered November ... leg wasn't easy to forget."

Summary: Snape confiscates Harry's *Quidditch through the Ages* book the day before the first Quidditch match of the season. Harry wants to get his book back, so he goes to the staffroom to find Snape. He knocks on the door, but no one answers. So he decides to have a look around in case the book's just sitting there. However, once he opens the door, he sees Filch tending to Snape's injured leg and runs back to the Gryffindor common room before he can get in trouble. Because of this, Harry's convinced that Snape let the troll in on Halloween, and that he's after whatever the three-headed dog is guarding on the third floor.

ANALYZING THE SCENE

STORY EVENT

A Story Event is an active change of a universal human value for one or more characters as a result of conflict (one character's desires clash with another's, or an environmental shift changes the value positively or negatively).

A Working Scene contains at least one Story Event. To determine a scene's Story Event, answer these four Socratic questions:

1. What are the characters literally doing—that is, what are their micro on-the-surface actions? Reader's Perspective (OTS)

Harry prepares for the Quidditch match and then tries to retrieve his book from the staffroom.
OTS Change (Harry): Common Room to Staffroom

2. What is the essential tactic of the characters—that is, what above-the-surface macro behaviors are they employing that are linked to a universal human value? Character's Perspective (ATS)

Snape wants Filch's help tending to his injured leg in private, but Harry wants his book back so he can continue preparing for the upcoming Quidditch match.
ATS Change (Harry): Sneaky to Seen / Risking Trouble to Caught

3. What beyond-the-surface universal human values have changed for one or more characters in the scene? Which one of those value changes is most important and should be included in the Story Grid Spreadsheet? Author's Perspective (BTS)

This is the first time Harry connects Snape to the mysterious package hidden on the third floor. He's convinced Snape let the troll into the castle to create a diversion so he could steal whatever's in the package, even though he doesn't know what it is or why Snape wants it. Although Harry has the right idea about *what's* going on (someone *is* trying to steal the package), he has the wrong suspect. And as long as Harry believes Snape is the bad guy, he's missing the real threat—Quirrell. And the closer Quirrell gets to the stone, the closer Voldemort comes to gain back his full power.

BTS Change (Harry): *Ignorance to Ignorance Masked as Knowledge*

4. The Scene Event Synthesis: What Story Event sums up the scene's on-the-surface, above-the-surface, and beyond-the-surface change? We will enter that event in the Story Grid Spreadsheet.

After eavesdropping on Filch tending to Snape's injured leg, Harry suspects Snape's trying to steal whatever the three-headed dog is guarding on the third floor.

HOW THE SCENE ABIDES BY THE FIVE COMMANDMENTS OF STORYTELLING

Inciting Incident: Causal. Snape confiscates Harry's book.

Turning Point Progressive Complication: Active. Harry knocks on the staffroom door but no one answers.

Crisis: Best Bad Choice. Should Harry enter the staffroom without permission and risk getting into trouble? Or should he give up and head back to the common room without his book?

Climax: Harry opens the door and sees Filch tending to Snape's injured leg.

Resolution: Harry races back up to the Gryffindor common room and tells Ron and Hermione what he just saw. He's convinced that Snape tried to get past the three-headed dog on Halloween and let the troll into the castle as a diversion. Ron agrees, but Hermione is skeptical.

NOTES

- This scene includes the Crisis of the Middle Buildup. Should Harry tell someone what knows about Snape, even if he might be wrong? Or should he keep his suspicions to himself and risk Snape succeeding in taking the package? Harry doesn't *really* have any proof to back up his decisions, so he can't do a whole lot except focus on the next immediate thing on the horizon—the Quidditch match against Slytherin.
- Did you catch how Ron and Hermione offer contrasting opinions about Snape that reflect one of the bigger lessons Harry learns in this book? Hermione says, "I know he's not very nice, but he wouldn't try and steal something Dumbledore was keeping safe." To which Ron says, "Honestly, Hermione, you think all teachers are saints or something." It's fun to see how a small conversation like this can reflect something much bigger. Harry must learn to trust his own judgments and rely on himself versus defaulting to the assumption that the adults know more than he does and/or are always right.
- It's interesting that Snape confiscates Harry's book based on a rule that we never see come up again in the series. Is this a mistake or an intentional way to show readers how far Snape will go to pick on Harry in his first year at Hogwarts? We may never know!

SCENE 15
QUIDDITCH
CHAPTER 11

2,392 words

"The next morning dawned very ... Hagrid looked furious with himself."

Summary: Someone jinxes Harry's broom during the Quidditch match against Slytherin. Luckily, Hermione saves Harry by setting Snape's cloak on fire and knocking Quirrell down in the process. Later, Harry, Ron, and Hermione share their suspicions about Snape with Hagrid, but Hagrid doesn't support their theory. Instead, he tells them to drop it and mentions that whatever the three-headed dog is guarding only concerns Dumbledore and Nicolas Flamel.

ANALYZING THE SCENE

STORY EVENT

A Story Event is an active change of a universal human value for one or more characters as a result of conflict (one character's desires clash with

another's, or an environmental shift changes the value positively or negatively).

A Working Scene contains at least one Story Event. To determine a scene's Story Event, answer these four Socratic questions:

1. **What are the characters literally doing—that is, what are their micro on-the-surface actions? Reader's Perspective (OTS)**

Harry participates in the Quidditch match against Slytherin and then Harry, Ron, and Hermione talk to Hagrid about their suspicions regarding Snape.

OTS Change (Harry): Quidditch Pitch to Hagrid's Hut

2. **What is the essential tactic of the characters—that is, what above-the-surface macro behaviors are they employing that are linked to a universal human value? Character's Perspective (ATS)**

Harry wants to win the Quidditch match against the Slytherins, but when someone jinxes his broom, his thoughts turn to survival. Hermione and Snape want to save Harry while Quirrell wants to take him down and likely kill him.

ATS Change (Harry): Suspicious to Convinced

3. **What beyond-the-surface universal human values have changed for one or more characters in the scene? Which one of those value changes is most important and should be included in the Story Grid Spreadsheet? Author's Perspective (BTS)**

This is the first time Quirrell directly targets Harry with the intention of killing him. Although Hermione and Snape physically protect Harry in this scene, he's not out of harm's way—especially now that he has another clue about what's in the package. If anything, Harry's escape makes him an even bigger threat and target to Quirrell. The more Harry digs into the truth about what's in the package and why Snape wants to steal it, the more he puts himself and his friends in danger. And now, Quirrell suspects that

Harry is investigating this mystery, which means eventually Harry might figure out Quirrell's scheme.

BTS Change (Harry): *Safe to Danger*

4. The Scene Event Synthesis: What Story Event sums up the scene's on-the-surface, above-the-surface, and beyond-the-surface change? We will enter that event in the Story Grid Spreadsheet.

Harry's suspicions that Snape is after whatever the three-headed dog is guarding are (seemingly) reaffirmed after someone (he assumes Snape) jinxes his broom during the Quidditch match.

HOW THE SCENE ABIDES BY THE FIVE COMMANDMENTS OF STORYTELLING

Inciting Incident: Causal. Harry loses control of his broom.

Turning Point Progressive Complication: Revelation. Hermione spots Snape in the crowd muttering nonstop under his breath and believes he's jinxing the broom.

Crisis: Best Bad Choice. Should Hermione do something to stop Snape from messing with Harry? Or should she stay out of it and risk Harry getting seriously injured or dying?

Climax: Hermione sets Snape's robes on fire, knocking Professor Quirrell over in the process.

Resolution: Later, Harry, Ron, and Hermione share their suspicions about Snape with Hagrid, but Hagrid doesn't support their theory. Hagrid tells them to drop it and that what the three-headed dog (Fluffy) is guarding only concerns Dumbledore and Nicolas Flamel.

NOTES

- This scene includes the Climax, and Resolution of the Middle Buildup and solidifies Harry's focus going into the Middle Breakdown. Now that someone has targeted and attacked him directly, Harry has to start taking more proactive action to stay safe.
- But what about the part in Hagrid's hut? Why isn't that a scene? You *could* say Harry faces a crisis in Hagrid's hut: Should he tell Hagrid everything he knows and suspects about Snape? Or keep his thoughts to himself? However, in that scenario, stakes are unclear. Is Harry *really* worried about sharing his thoughts with Hagrid? Probably not. Conversely, you could infer a crisis from Hagrid's point of view as well: Should he tell the kids what he knows to assuage their worries or stay silent? But that's not on the page either. Plus, it's a very small part of the scene at only three hundred words!
- Notice how Rowling sets up Snape as the red herring in this scene. Hermione knocks Professor Quirrell over on her way to set fire to Snape's robes. Knocking Professor Quirrell over interrupts the curse, but we don't find that out until later. Rowling put Snape and Quirrell in a scene together (again) to allow the reader (and Harry, Ron, and Hermione) to think Snape's the bad guy, and it works!
- Harry catches the Golden Snitch in his mouth. This setup pays off later in book seven, *Harry Potter and the Deathly Hallows*, when Dumbledore gives Harry the same Golden Snitch with a mysterious note that says, "I open at the close." Although we can't know for sure whether Rowling had this connection planned from book one, it's fun to think about how an author can bring back seemingly insignificant details from previous books to create full circle moments like this.
- Hagrid mentions only powerful Dark magic could interfere with a broom. Hermione associates this with Professor Snape (likely because everyone knows he loves the Dark Arts) even though Professor Quirrell is the Defense Against the Dark Arts teacher.

Because we're limited to what Harry and his friends know, it's easy to believe their subjective interpretation of events. This is the power of point of view!

- Speaking of point of view, did you notice the slight shift in this scene? Rowling briefly zooms out of Harry's perspective and zooms into Hermione's point of view (although not as close) for a few paragraphs. The switch is so subtle that it's easy to miss as a reader. But if we think about why Rowling did this, it makes sense because Harry is flying high in the air above the Quidditch pitch, unable to save himself. Rowling lets us experience what's happening to Harry over Hermione's shoulder since she's the one to take action and save Harry's life. As such, Hermione owns the scene crisis, making the all-important climax decision that saves Harry's life.

SCENE 16
THE MIRROR OF ERISED
CHAPTER 12

5,478 words

"Christmas was coming. One morning ... been quite a personal question."

Summary: Despite their best efforts, Harry, Ron, and Hermione fail to find more information on Nicolas Flamel. However, during Christmas break, Harry receives an Invisibility Cloak that he later uses to investigate the Restricted Section of the library for clues. Unfortunately, he's almost caught by Snape and Filch but manages to outrun them by escaping into an unused classroom. There, he sees a giant mirror, and when he approaches the mirror, he sees his parents reflected back to him in the glass. The next night, Harry shows Ron the mirror, but Ron sees something different. He sees himself as Head Boy and the Quidditch Captain who won Gryffindor the House Cup. Afterward, Ron tells Harry to stop going back to the mirror because of a bad feeling about it, but Harry continues to visit the mirror. Eventually, Dumbledore catches Harry, tells him how the mirror works, and asks Harry not to look for the mirror again before moving it to a different location in the school.

ANALYZING THE SCENE

STORY EVENT

A Story Event is an active change of a universal human value for one or more characters as a result of conflict (one character's desires clash with another's, or an environmental shift changes the value positively or negatively).

A Working Scene contains at least one Story Event. To determine a scene's Story Event, answer these four Socratic questions:

1. What are the characters literally doing—that is, what are their micro on-the-surface actions? Reader's Perspective (OTS)

Harry, Ron, and Hermione finish up their classes and go on Christmas break. Harry and Ron stay at Hogwarts while Hermione goes on vacation with her parents.
OTS Change (Harry): School in Session to Christmas Holiday

2. What is the essential tactic of the characters—that is, what above-the-surface macro behaviors are they employing that are linked to a universal human value? Character's Perspective (ATS)

Before Christmas break, Harry, Ron, and Hermione are determined to find information on Nicolas Flamel. However, once Christmas break starts, Harry and Ron become distracted by all the merriment. After receiving an Invisibility Cloak, Harry resumes the hunt for information in the Restricted Section of the library but ends up accidentally finding the Mirror of Erised instead. His focus shifts again from finding information on Flamel to "spending time with" his family. Dumbledore, however, wants to hide the Mirror of Erised to protect Harry from becoming obsessed with it.
ATS Change (Harry): Focused to Distracted / Tempted to Spared

3. What beyond-the-surface universal human values have changed for one or more characters in the scene? Which one of those value changes

is most important and should be included in the Story Grid Spreadsheet? Author's Perspective (BTS)

Harry receives gifts that will help him succeed in and survive the upcoming conflict: a flute from Hagrid (he'll use this later when they go through the trapdoor), Chocolate Frogs from Hermione (he'll learn about the connection between Nicolas Flamel and the Sorcerer's Stone from one of these Chocolate Frog cards later), a Weasley sweater from Ron's family (giving him the sense of family and belonging he's been lacking), lessons in wizard chess from Ron (a skill that comes into play once they go through the trapdoor), and an Invisibility Cloak from Dumbledore. He also discovers the Mirror of Erised. Although Harry is tempted by his longing (if not growing obsession) to have his parents alive again, he also has an intimate teaching experience from his mentor, Dumbledore. This prepares Harry to not be tempted by his own desires later when facing Voldemort and Quirrell and allows him to understand how the mirror works.

BTS Change (Harry): *Unequipped to Equipped*

4. The Scene Event Synthesis: What Story Event sums up the scene's on-the-surface, above-the-surface, and beyond-the-surface change? We will enter that event in the Story Grid Spreadsheet.

Harry uses the invisibility cloak to hunt down information on Nicolas Flamel but becomes distracted by the Mirror of Erised instead.

HOW THE SCENE ABIDES BY THE FIVE COMMANDMENTS OF STORYTELLING

Inciting Incident: Causal. Harry receives an invisibility cloak for Christmas.

Turning Point Progressive Complication: Active. While using the Invisibility Cloak to look for information on Nicolas Flamel, Harry discovers the Mirror of Erised.

Crisis: Best Bad Choice. Should Harry listen to Ron and stay away from the mirror even if that means not seeing his parents anymore? Or should he continue visiting the mirror and risk getting caught and losing points for Gryffindor (or worse)?

Climax: Harry keeps visiting the mirror despite Ron's warnings.

Resolution: Dumbledore catches Harry visiting the mirror, tells Harry he's going to move the mirror, and asks Harry not to try to find it again. As a result of all of this, Harry has failed to find any information on Nicolas Flamel.

NOTES

- If you look at the big picture of this scene, Harry, Ron, and Hermione's goal is to find information on Nicolas Flamel. The smaller moments within the overarching scene and inside some of the narrative summary that covers about a month and a half serve as Progressive Complications, making it more and more difficult for Harry to focus on his goal. When the scene starts, the kids *are* looking for information on Flamel, but then Hermione leaves, and the Christmas holiday starts, distracting Harry and Ron from their research. The conflict deepens once Harry finds the Mirror of Erised and chooses to focus on "spending time with" his family rather than finding information on Flamel. That being said, when planning and writing your own stories, feel free to break up moments like this as if they were each one a "scene" with their own set of Five Commandments. You can always re-evaluate things once you get to the editing stage.
- Harry's sense of belonging (and found family) is secured here, and it gives Harry something to fight for when he faces Voldemort at the end. At the same time, it reinforces what Harry lacks and desires above all else: a family and a home. Harry

wants a family and a home so badly that he's willing to give up his quest to find more information on Nicolas Flamel to sit in front of the mirror and stare at his parents. This is a great way to "show" what a character wants (or longs for) without being overly direct about it.

- Harry doesn't know the Invisibility Cloak came from Dumbledore, but he finds out in the last chapter. Dumbledore's trust in Harry to "use it well" pays off when Harry succeeds in preventing Voldemort from getting the Sorcerer's Stone.
- Consider how Snape interferes when Malfoy taunts Ron and Harry for staying at the school over the holidays. When Ron reacts (diving for Malfoy), Snape chooses to focus on Ron's actions versus what Malfoy did to incite the situation. Because of this, Snape takes points from Gryffindor, but not Slytherin. Even though this is unfair, it shows us (and Harry) that actions have consequences—and throughout the Middle Breakdown, we'll see Harry's actions cost Gryffindor more and more points until ultimately he and his friends lose 150 points *each* for helping Norbert escape. As you read the next section, notice how Rowling uses moments like this to "break down" Harry and his reputation at the school.
- Fred and George Weasley get punished for throwing snowballs at the back of Quirrell's turban. What we don't yet realize is that they're actually throwing snowballs right at Voldemort! Rowling often uses Fred and George as a way to inject humor into the story and hide clues behind their humor, even if readers don't catch it right away.
- This chapter includes another mention of Charlie being in Romania, where the dragons are. This small mention of Charlie allows Rowling to touch on the "dragon" subplot without including too much unnecessary information. Doing this allows Harry's future plan to relocate Norbert to feel like an organic part of the story because Charlie and his connection to dragons has been mentioned so many times.
- Professor Snape wants to know if anyone (Quirrell) has visited the Restricted Section of the library where books on Dark Magic

are stored. Harry assumes Snape's talking about him having been in the Restricted Section (because who else would Harry think he's talking about), and we trust Harry's interpretation of what's happening because we're limited to seeing things from his perspective. This allows Rowling to use Snape as the red herring to distract us from the truth about Quirrell again and again.

- "Erised" is "desire" written backward. The inscription says, "I show not your face but your heart's desire." This is a great setup (and clue) for later when Harry looks in the mirror and his only desire is for Quirrell/Voldemort to not get the stone—for the stone to be safe. It's also interesting because, like a patronus (a silver, animal guardian, used to protect a witch or wizard against Dementors), the image in the mirror can change based on how you grow and change as a person. For example, Harry first sees his parents in the mirror but then sees the stone in the global Climax. Details like this help Rowling show Harry's growth over time, whether in this book or throughout the series.

- Did you notice how Ron mentions liking Harry's sweater better than his own. For some reason, Ron perceives Harry's sweater to be better than the one he received. This hints at Ron's internal obstacle. He's always comparing himself (and what he has, or has accomplished) to others (and what they have, or have accomplished) and finding himself "less than." When he looks in the mirror, Ron sees himself as Head Boy, Quidditch Captain, and winner of the Quidditch Cup. This shows that Ron does not have his own definition of success. Instead, he wants to succeed in the same way all of his brothers before him have succeeded. To Ron, that's how he will feel self-worth. And this is something major that Ron will have to work on throughout the series. By the end of the series, Ron has really gone above and beyond anything his brothers have accomplished by playing a huge part in Harry's quest to take down Voldemort.

- Dumbledore delivers a fan favorite quote in this scene, "It does not do to dwell on dreams and forget to live." This is a great reminder for all readers, whether they can directly relate to

Harry's exact experience in this scene or not, and it aptly expresses the lesson Harry learns in this scene, too.
- In a 2005 interview with MuggleNet and the Leaky Cauldron, Rowling stated that if Voldemort had discovered the mirror, he would see, "Himself, all-powerful and eternal. That's what he wants." Voldemort is a great antagonist case study because his goal *is* very clear from the start. He wants power and immortality and will destroy anyone who gets in his way—wizard and Muggle alike. This continues to be true and consistent throughout the series, though his tactics for gaining immortality and power change from book to book.

SCENE 17
NICOLAS FLAMEL

CHAPTER 13

1,618 words

"Dumbledore had convinced Harry not ... that Snape could read minds."

Summary: Once school starts again, Harry, Ron, and Hermione continue the search for information on Nicolas Flamel but have no luck. Quidditch season is almost over, and Harry is hoping that Gryffindor will win the next match against Hufflepuff so they can overtake Slytherin in the House Championship. However, once he learns that Snape's going to referee the match, he's not sure if it's a good idea to play lest someone jinx his broom again. After discussing his options with Ron and Hermione, helping Neville out of a Leg-Locker Curse, and accidentally discovering that Nicolas Flamel was the creator of the Sorcerer's Stone, Harry is determined to play in the Quidditch match to prove to the Slytherins he's not afraid of Snape.

ANALYZING THE SCENE

STORY EVENT

A Story Event is an active change of a universal human value for one or more characters as a result of conflict (one character's desires clash with another's, or an environmental shift changes the value positively or negatively).

A Working Scene contains at least one Story Event. To determine a scene's Story Event, answer these four Socratic questions:

1. **What are the characters literally doing—that is, what are their micro on-the-surface actions? Reader's Perspective (OTS)**

Harry practices and prepares for the upcoming Quidditch match and talks to his friends.
OTS Change (Harry): Quidditch Pitch to Castle

2. **What is the essential tactic of the characters—that is, what above-the-surface macro behaviors are they employing that are linked to a universal human value? Character's Perspective (ATS)**

Snape wants to keep Harry safe during the upcoming Quidditch match, so he volunteers to referee. When Harry learns Snape will be refereeing the match, he debates not participating to keep himself out of harm's way but ultimately decides that he *will* play, if only to keep the Slytherins from thinking he's a coward.
ATS Change (Harry): Nervous to Brave

3. **What beyond-the-surface universal human values have changed for one or more characters in the scene? Which one of those value changes is most important and should be included in the Story Grid Spreadsheet? Author's Perspective (BTS)**

There's no going back for Harry after he learns that Nicolas Flamel created the Sorcerer's Stone. From here on out, he'll risk getting in trouble and even dying to keep the stone safe. This knowledge of *what's* being kept on the third floor ups the stakes for Harry because he doesn't want Snape to gain immortality. However, although he *suspects* Snape wants to steal it, he doesn't have any proof.

BTS Change (Harry): *Ignorance to Knowledge*

4. The Scene Event Synthesis: What Story Event sums up the scene's on-the-surface, above-the-surface, and beyond-the-surface change? We will enter that event in the Story Grid Spreadsheet.

Harry, Ron, and Hermione learn that Nicolas Flamel created the Sorcerer's Stone and realize that's what's being kept hidden on the third floor.

HOW THE SCENE ABIDES BY THE FIVE COMMANDMENTS OF STORYTELLING

Inciting Incident: Causal. Harry learns Snape's going to referee the upcoming Quidditch match.

Turning Point Progressive Complication: Active. Ron and Hermione urge Harry not to play.

Crisis: Best Bad Choice. Should Harry play in the match even though he believes Snape's out to get him? Or should he bow out, causing Gryffindor to forfeit their chance at the House Championship?

Climax: Harry decides he will play.

Resolution: Right after Harry decides to play, Neville topples into the Gryffindor common room and the kids help him out of the Leg-Locker Curse that's stuck his legs together. On his way out, Neville gives Harry a Chocolate Frog card that contains information they've been desperately seeking. Nicolas Flamel created the Sorcerer's Stone. Harry is convinced that *this* is what's in the package on the third floor—and what Snape wants to steal—but he lacks proof.

NOTES

- This scene contains the Inciting Incident of the Middle Breakdown. Now that Harry knows exactly *what's* hidden on the third floor, he's determined to prevent Snape from getting it. This is his goal for most of the Middle Breakdown. However, he still lacks proof, so he can't do much about what he suspects.
- The global story advances when Harry, Ron, and Hermione learn who Nicolas Flamel is but notice that the Five Commandments of Storytelling are built around the Quidditch match. This is a good example of a scene to model when you need to include important plot information but don't want or need to build a scene around that information. In other words, this scene is built (and moves) around Harry's decision to play Quidditch, but Rowling was still able to organically include the reveal that Nicolas Flamel created the Sorcerer's Stone, which moves the global story forward.
- Notice that Harry, Ron, and Hermione had to become friends and work together to discover the clue hidden in the Chocolate Frog card. The last Chocolate Frog from Hermione's Christmas present holds the answers about Nicolas Flamel and the Sorcerer's Stone. Fun fact: Did you know that Nicolas Flamel and his wife, Perenelle, are real people in history? Pretty cool!
- In this scene, we hear the first mention of Dumbledore defeating a dark wizard named Grindelwald. This feels like a throwaway detail, but it's a large part of Dumbledore's backstory that we learn more about later in book seven, *Harry Potter and the Deathly Hallows*.
- Harry keeps running into Snape wherever he goes. He wonders if Snape is following him and even has "the horrible feeling that Snape could read minds." In later books, we learn that Snape *can* read minds as he's an Occlumens. Snape gives Harry lessons in Occlumency in book five, *Harry Potter and the Order of the Phoenix*.

- This is a great scene to read again once you realize Snape isn't the bad guy. Harry feels scared and threatened when he learns that Snape's refereeing the Quidditch match, but he's actually there for Harry's protection. By limiting the point of view to just one character (Harry), Rowling is able to misdirect the reader's attention because we can only know and experience what Harry does. If we could see inside of Snape's head (like we do Harry's), this scene would be less impactful.
- It's strange that the school would allow Snape, the head of Slytherin, to referee the match since Gryffindor winning would knock Slytherin out of first place. And even stranger that either Snape or Dumbledore must have requested this substitution as Madam Hooch is the flying teacher and routine referee. Although a small detail, this gives readers a clue that things might not be quite as they seem.
- Harry's having nightmares about the night his parents died. He sees a flash of green light and hears a high voice cackling with laughter. We don't know what this means yet, but it's a great example of choosing details with purpose. Instead of inserting a random dream that has the same emotional effect on Harry, Rowling pulled from what she already had available in the story and used it as a way to tell us (without literally telling us) what happened to Harry's parents. Also, did you notice how she reveals more and more of the backstory over time? In chapter seven "The Sorting Hat," she only mentioned "a burst of green light," but here, we get a little more detail. This is a great way to "drip feed" information to readers without overwhelming them or info-dumping.

SCENE 18
NICOLAS FLAMEL
CHAPTER 13

1,560 words

"Harry knew, when they wished ... by next Tuesday," said Ron."

Summary: After winning the Quidditch match, Harry sees Snape creep down the front steps of the castle and decides to follow him into the Forbidden Forest. He eavesdrops on a conversation in which Snape seemingly threatens Quirrell for information about getting past Fluffy and races back to the castle to tell his friends what he heard.

ANALYZING THE SCENE

STORY EVENT

A Story Event is an active change of a universal human value for one or more characters as a result of conflict (one character's desires clash with another's, or an environmental shift changes the value positively or negatively).

A Working Scene contains at least one Story Event. To determine a scene's Story Event, answer these four Socratic questions:

1. What are the characters literally doing—that is, what are their micro on-the-surface actions? Reader's Perspective (OTS)

Harry participates in a Quidditch match and eavesdrops on Snape and Quirrell.
OTS Change (Harry): Quidditch Pitch to Forbidden Forest

2. What is the essential tactic of the characters—that is, what above-the-surface macro behaviors are they employing that are linked to a universal human value? Character's Perspective (ATS)

Harry needs proof that what he suspects about Snape is true, so he follows him into the Forbidden Forest that he *knows* is off limits to students. Snape wants to stop Quirrell from pursuing the Sorcerer's Stone, but Harry misinterprets their conversation and takes this as proof that Snape is going after the stone himself.
ATS Change (Harry): Suspicious to Convinced / Lacking Evidence to Proof

3. What beyond-the-surface universal human values have changed for one or more characters in the scene? Which one of those value changes is most important and should be included in the Story Grid Spreadsheet? Author's Perspective (BTS)

Harry follows Snape into the Forbidden Forest, which he *knows* is dangerous and off-limits to students. However, he's determined to figure out what Snape is up to and to find proof that he's after the Sorcerer's Stone. As long as Harry believes Snape is the threat, Harry overlooks the danger Quirrell creates, and thus, allows Quirrell to get closer to acquiring the stone for Voldemort, which would result in Voldemort coming back to full power.
BTS Change (Harry): *Safe to Danger*

4. **The Scene Event Synthesis:** What Story Event sums up the scene's on-the-surface, above-the-surface, and beyond-the-surface change? We will enter that event in the Story Grid Spreadsheet.

Harry spies on Snape and Quirrell in the Forbidden Forest and interprets their conversation as proof that Snape's going to steal the Sorcerer's Stone.

HOW THE SCENE ABIDES BY THE FIVE COMMANDMENTS OF STORYTELLING

Inciting Incident: Causal. Harry and Ron notice that Snape seems upset about Dumbledore's presence at the Quidditch match.

Turning Point Progressive Complication: Active. After the match, Harry sees Snape leave the castle and head to the Forbidden Forest.

Crisis: Best Bad Choice. Should Harry follow Snape into the Forbidden Forest and risk getting into trouble and possibly endangering himself? Or should he head up to dinner and miss this chance to spy on Snape and possibly learn the truth about what he's up to?

Climax: Harry jumps on his broom and follows Snape into the forest.

Resolution: Harry eavesdrops on Professors Snape and Quirrell and interprets what he hears as proof that Snape wants to steal the Sorcerer's Stone. Ron and Hermione worry about Quirrell's ability to protect the stone and do their best to encourage and protect him from the sidelines.

NOTES

- This scene offers a great example of how you can have value shifts on multiple levels to create an impactful scene. First, Harry plays in the Quidditch match even though Snape will be refereeing. From Harry's (and the reader's) perspective, this puts Harry in danger *until* Dumbledore shows up in the stands. Later, when Harry follows Snape into the Forbidden Forest, which he *knows* is off-limits to students, he puts himself in *actual* danger.

- This scene solidifies Snape as the red herring. On the surface, it seems like Snape is angry because Gryffindor is now in the lead for winning the House Cup or because he failed to harm Harry during the match. But it's possible that Snape's angry because he feels duty bound to protect Harry while Quirrell's free to roam the castle and possibly steal the stone while everyone's busy with the match. Either way you look at it (whether you know the truth about Snape or not) his actions are believable, and that's the key to writing an effective red herring.

- Did you notice Rowling zooms out to an omniscient perspective for (a very small) part of this scene? Once the match starts, we leave Harry's perspective and dip into a moment between Hermione, Ron, Neville, Malfoy, Crabbe, and Goyle. This shift in perspective happens so quickly that it's easy to miss, but it makes sense because the on-the-ground excitement is likely much more interesting than following Harry as he catches the snitch.

SCENE 19

NORBERT THE NORWEGIAN RIDGEBACK

CHAPTER 14

2,172 words

"Quirrell, however, must have been ... to Charlie to ask him"

Summary: With their end-of-year exams approaching, Harry, Ron, and Hermione dedicate themselves to studying. However, when they learn that Hagrid's hatching an illegal dragon in his hut, they turn their attention to helping Hagrid stay out of trouble. Unfortunately, Draco Malfoy sees the dragon hatch, and Harry, Ron, and Hermione know it's only a matter of time until he uses that information to get Hagrid in trouble. So, they get in touch with Charlie, Ron's brother, and ask for help in relocating Norbert.

ANALYZING THE SCENE

STORY EVENT

A Story Event is an active change of a universal human value for one or more characters as a result of conflict (one character's desires clash with

another's, or an environmental shift changes the value positively or negatively).

A Working Scene contains at least one Story Event. To determine a scene's Story Event, answer these four Socratic questions:

1. What are the characters literally doing—that is, what are their micro on-the-surface actions? Reader's Perspective (OTS)

Harry, Ron, and Hermione study in the library and then visit Hagrid's to watch his dragon egg hatch.

OTS Change (Harry): Library to Hagrid's hut / Studying to Watching Egg Hatch

2. What is the essential tactic of the characters—that is, what above-the-surface macro behaviors are they employing that are linked to a universal human value? Character's Perspective (ATS)

Harry, Ron, and Hermione want to know more about what's guarding the Sorcerer's Stone, so when Hagrid invites them to his hut to speak about it in private, they're thrilled! However, Hagrid isn't supposed to tell anyone what he knows, so he does his best to assure the kids the stone is safe while not breaking his promise to Dumbledore.

ATS Change (Harry): Worried to Relieved

3. What beyond-the-surface universal human values have changed for one or more characters in the scene? Which one of those value changes is most important and should be included in the Story Grid Spreadsheet? Author's Perspective (BTS)

After Harry, Ron, and Hermione learn that many safety features are in place to keep the Sorcerer's Stone safe, they focus on a new problem. Hagrid has hatched an illegal dragon in his very flammable hut, and Malfoy saw everything! If the kids don't help Hagrid, he'll likely get fired (maybe even arrested), but if they do help Hagrid, they'll be risking danger (and maybe even expulsion).

BTS Change (Harry): *Safe to Safety Threatened*

4. **The Scene Event Synthesis:** What Story Event sums up the scene's on-the-surface, above-the-surface, and beyond-the-surface change? We will enter that event in the Story Grid Spreadsheet.

> *Hagrid reassures the kids that the Sorcerer's Stone is safe, but now they have a new problem—relocating the illegal dragon Hagrid hatched!*

HOW THE SCENE ABIDES BY THE FIVE COMMANDMENTS OF STORYTELLING

Inciting Incident: Causal. Harry, Ron, and Hermione learn that Hagrid has a dragon egg.

Turning Point Progressive Complication: Revelatory. Harry realizes Malfoy was spying through the window and saw the dragon hatch.

Crisis: Best Bad Choice. Should Harry, Ron, and Hermione help Hagrid get rid of his dragon and risk getting into trouble? Or should they mind their own business and risk Hagrid getting into trouble once Malfoy tells on him?

Climax: They decide to help Hagrid.

Resolution: They send a note to Ron's brother, Charlie, asking for help relocating the dragon.

NOTES

- Although this scene spans multiple locations, everything adds up to one primary arc of change and value shift: Hagrid hatches an illegal dragon and the kids decide to help him relocate it. The smaller moments within this scene serve as Progressive Complications that increase the conflict and tension and raise the stakes. By the end of this scene, Harry's decision to help Hagrid gives rise to the goal in the next scene—to get rid of Norbert without getting caught.

- This scene might feel like the beginning to a side quest, especially considering Harry, Ron, and Hermione have just begun unraveling the truth about Nicolas Flamel and the Sorcerer's Stone, but it lays important groundwork for the rest of the book (and series). Specifically, this draws the spotlight back to Harry and Malfoy's growing animosity, which reaches its peak in this chapter. It's also a fun and effective way for the author to set Harry up to serve detention in the Forbidden Forest, where he learns the truth about Voldemort, in chapter fifteen, "The Forbidden Forest."

- Hagrid explains to Harry, Ron, and Hermione how multiple teachers are responsible for guarding the Sorcerer's Stone—including Snape. This is a setup for what comes later in chapter sixteen, "Through the Trapdoor," when the kids have to pass each teacher's test or obstacle to reach the final chamber.

- This scene shows us that the traits associated with each house are not black and white. Hagrid was sorted into Gryffindor, but in this scene he's acting more like a Hufflepuff as he nurtures and tends to Norbert. Hermione is also a Gryffindor but has many traits associated with Ravenclaw (her intelligence, wit, and level-headedness). This gives us an important clue for the entire series—you can't judge someone based on their school house—and this clue is paid off when we finally learn the truth about Snape.

SCENE 20
NORBERT THE NORWEGIAN RIDGEBACK
CHAPTER 14

1,911 words

"The following week dragged by ... found out what they'd done?"

Summary: The following week, Harry and Hermione successfully escort Norbert to the top of the tallest tower and hand him off to Charlie. However, Professor McGonagall catches them and gives Harry, Hermione, Neville, and Malfoy detention. Not only that, but they each lose fifty points, putting Gryffindor in last place and ruining their chance at winning the House Cup.

ANALYZING THE SCENE

STORY EVENT

A Story Event is an active change of a universal human value for one or more characters as a result of conflict (one character's desires clash with another's, or an environmental shift changes the value positively or negatively).

A Working Scene contains at least one Story Event. To determine a scene's Story Event, answer these four Socratic questions:

1. What are the characters literally doing—that is, what are their micro on-the-surface actions? Reader's Perspective (OTS)

   Harry and Hermione work together to hand Norbert off to Charlie's friends.
   OTS Change (Harry): Common Room to Tallest Tower

2. What is the essential tactic of the characters—that is, what above-the-surface macro behaviors are they employing that are linked to a universal human value? Character's Perspective (ATS)

   Harry, Ron, and Hermione want to help Hagrid rehome his dragon so he doesn't get in trouble. Malfoy wants to get Harry in trouble or even better, expelled.
   ATS Change (Harry): Burdened (by Norbert) to Relieved (of Norbert) / Sneaky to Caught

3. What beyond-the-surface universal human values have changed for one or more characters in the scene? Which one of those value changes is most important and should be included in the Story Grid Spreadsheet? Author's Perspective (BTS)

   Harry will always put his neck out for his friends, and he does this for Hagrid at the risk of getting in trouble, or worse, finding himself in some serious danger. Even though he's successful in relocating Norbert, he ends the scene in a lot of trouble. His actions have put Gryffindor in last place and taken the wind out of his sails in terms of his desire to protect the Sorcerer's Stone.
   BTS Change (Harry): *Risking Trouble to In Trouble*

4. The Scene Event Synthesis: What Story Event sums up the scene's on-the-surface, above-the-surface, and beyond-the-surface change? We will enter that event in the Story Grid Spreadsheet.

Harry, Ron, and Hermione successfully help Hagrid relocate his illegal dragon but get detention and lose 150 points for Gryffindor as a result.

HOW THE SCENE ABIDES BY THE FIVE COMMANDMENTS OF STORYTELLING

Inciting Incident: Causal. Charlie writes back and says some of his friends can pick up Norbert this Saturday if Harry, Ron, and Hermione can get him to the top of the tallest tower.

Turning Point Progressive Complication: Revelatory. Ron remembers that Charlie's letter was in that book Malfoy took, so he'll know they're helping Hagrid get rid of Norbert.

Crisis: Best Bad Choice. Should they change the plan to avoid Malfoy's interference but risk Norbert hurting someone or worse? Or should they stick to the plan and use the Invisibility Cloak to hide themselves in case of interference?

Climax: They decide it's too late to change the plan.

Resolution: Harry and Hermione bring Norbert to the tallest tower and successfully hand him off to Charlie's friends but get detention as a result.

NOTES

- This scene is the Turning Point of the Middle Breakdown. After risking physical danger and possibly expulsion to help Hagrid relocate Norbert, the kids get detention. Harry's in the most trouble he's ever been in since coming to Hogwarts, and his actions have dropped Gryffindor into last place. He's gone from one of the most popular first-years to the most disliked. Not only that, but his friends are suffering too. Hermione has stopped speaking out in class, nobody's talking to Neville (who was already unpopular), and Ron's an outcast by association.

- McGonagall's punishment is interesting because I doubt Harry, Hermione, Neville, and Malfoy are the *only* kids to be caught out of bed after hours. The fact that her punishment is so harsh is a clue that the teachers might be more aware of the threat to the Sorcerer's Stone than we realize. McGonagall says, "*Nothing* gives you the right to walk around school at night, especially these days, it's very dangerous," yet there's been no mention of a rising threat in the wizarding world thus far, so what is she talking about? Is her warning simply due to the fact that the forest *is* full of dangerous creatures? Or is she more aware of the threat to the Sorcerer's Stone than we realize?

SCENE 21
NORBERT THE NORWEGIAN RIDGEBACK
CHAPTER 14

879 words

"At first, Gryffindors passing the ... the name of its moons."

Summary: Harry is so defeated by what happened during Norbert's escape that he can't even bring himself to get involved when he sees Snape confronting Quirrell in an empty classroom. Hermione suggests they tell Dumbledore, but Harry knows they don't have enough proof.

ANALYZING THE SCENE

STORY EVENT

A Story Event is an active change of a universal human value for one or more characters as a result of conflict (one character's desires clash with another's, or an environmental shift changes the value positively or negatively).

A Working Scene contains at least one Story Event. To determine a scene's Story Event, answer these four Socratic questions:

1. What are the characters literally doing—that is, what are their micro on-the-surface actions? Reader's Perspective (OTS)

Harry tells Hermione and Ron that he overheard someone threatening Quirrell.
OTS Change (Harry): Hogwarts Castle to Library

2. What is the essential tactic of the characters—that is, what above-the-surface macro behaviors are they employing that are linked to a universal human value? Character's Perspective (ATS)

Harry wants to avoid getting into any more trouble, but when he overhears someone threatening Quirrell, he's tempted to step in, especially when Hermione and Ron encourage him to do something about what he heard. However, Harry is determined to stay out of it.
ATS Change (Harry): Depressed to Indifferent / Public Hero to Public Disappointment

3. What beyond-the-surface universal human values have changed for one or more characters in the scene? Which one of those value changes is most important and should be included in the Story Grid Spreadsheet? Author's Perspective (BTS)

Harry no longer wants to risk getting into trouble, which makes it more likely he'll play the role of bystander versus hero. If Harry remains defeated, and fails to step into his role as The Boy Who Lived, Quirrell will succeed in acquiring the stone for Voldemort.
BTS Change (Harry): *Safe to Risking Danger*

4. The Scene Event Synthesis: What Story Event sums up the scene's on-the-surface, above-the-surface, and beyond-the-surface change? We will enter that event in the Story Grid Spreadsheet.

Harry believes Quirrell has finally told Snape how to get past Fluffy to secure the stone, however he's not willing to risk getting into more trouble to prevent that from happening.

HOW THE SCENE ABIDES BY THE FIVE COMMANDMENTS OF STORYTELLING

Inciting Incident: Causal. Harry overhears someone threatening Quirrell.

Turning Point Progressive Complication: Action. Harry tells Ron and Hermione what he overheard and saw and that he suspects Quirrell has finally told Snape how to get past Fluffy. Hermione suggests they tell Dumbledore.

Crisis: Best Bad Choice. Should they go to Dumbledore even though they have zero proof that Snape's done anything wrong? Or should they stay out of it to avoid getting into even more trouble?

Climax: Harry decides to stay out of it.

Resolution: Harry is determined to stay out of trouble after going from being one of the most admired students (for his Quidditch win) to one of the most disliked (for losing points and putting Gryffindor in last place).

NOTES

- This is the Crisis of the Middle Breakdown. After the events of the last scene, Harry's feeling really defeated. If he goes to Dumbledore with what he *thinks* he knows about Snape, this could get him into more trouble, or even worse, expelled. But if he doesn't, and what he suspects is true, they're all in danger.
- Did you notice Quirrell exited the classroom straightening his turban? This is a fun little clue about who he was *really* talking to. (Hint: It wasn't Snape!)

SCENE 22

THE FORBIDDEN FOREST

CHAPTER 15

3,576 words

"The following morning, notes were ... to it, "Just in case."

Summary: Harry, Hermione, Neville, and Malfoy serve detention in the Forbidden Forest. Hagrid splits them into groups and instructs each to find the injured, or possibly dead, unicorn. Harry and Malfoy find the unicorn with a hooded figure looming over it drinking its blood. Malfoy and Fang run away, but Harry stays put. His scar explodes in pain when the figure looks at him (and later moves to attack him), but Firenze (a centaur) steps in and saves Harry's life. On the way back to the castle, Firenze tells Harry the value and cost of drinking unicorn blood, and because of this, Harry realizes that the only person who would need unicorn blood is Lord Voldemort. Back in the Gryffindor common room, Harry tells Ron and Hermione that he now believes Snape wants to steal the stone *for* Voldemort.

ANALYZING THE SCENE

STORY EVENT

A Story Event is an active change of a universal human value for one or more characters as a result of conflict (one character's desires clash with another's, or an environmental shift changes the value positively or negatively).

A Working Scene contains at least one Story Event. To determine a scene's Story Event, answer these four Socratic questions:

1. What are the characters literally doing—that is, what are their micro on-the-surface actions? Reader's Perspective (OTS)

Harry, Hermione, Neville, and Malfoy serve detention with Hagrid in the Forbidden Forest by helping him find an injured unicorn.
OTS Change: Hogwarts to Forbidden Forest / Eating Breakfast to Serving Detention

2. What is the essential tactic of the characters—that is, what above-the-surface macro behaviors are they employing that are linked to a universal human value? Character's Perspective (ATS)

Harry, Hermione, and Neville want to help Hagrid find the unicorn so they can finish their detention and so Hagrid can finally figure out what's harming the unicorns. The hooded figure wants to kill and drink the unicorn blood in order to survive and later wants to kill Harry.
ATS Change (Harry): Wary to Terrified

3. What beyond-the-surface universal human values have changed for one or more characters in the scene? Which one of those value changes is most important and should be included in the Story Grid Spreadsheet? Author's Perspective (BTS)

Harry and the other students are unaware of the severity of danger in the forest—Voldemort. Even though Firenze rescues Harry from Voldemort, he's still not completely safe. Voldemort is getting closer and closer to the stone. As long as Harry continues to misjudge Snape and misinterpret his actions, he leaves himself exposed to threats like Quirrell/Voldemort.

BTS Change (Harry): *Risking Danger to Danger Realized*

4. The Scene Event Synthesis: What Story Event sums up the scene's on-the-surface, above-the-surface, and beyond-the-surface change? We will enter that event in the Story Grid Spreadsheet.

While serving detention in the Forbidden Forest, Harry learns that the hooded figure who's been killing unicorns is actually Voldemort, and Snape must want the Sorcerer's Stone to help Voldemort come back to life/power.

HOW THE SCENE ABIDES BY THE FIVE COMMANDMENTS OF STORYTELLING

Inciting Incident: Causal. A note from McGonagall arrives telling Harry and Hermione their detention is tonight and to meet Mr. Filch in the entrance hall.

Turning Point Progressive Complication: Active. Harry sees a hooded figure drinking the unicorn's blood, and his scar erupts in pain.

Crisis: Best Bad Choice. Should Harry attempt to fight the slithering figure or should he run?

Climax: Harry freezes; he cannot move for fear.

Resolution: Firenze scares off the hooded figure, saving Harry's life. After speaking with Firenze about what happened, Harry realizes the hooded figure was none other than Lord Voldemort himself, and Snape must want the Sorcerer's Stone to give to Voldemort so he can come back to life/power.

NOTES

- This is the global Turning Point of the story and the Climax and Resolution of the Middle Breakdown. This scene moves Harry closer to danger in multiple ways. First, he's serving detention in one of the most dangerous locations at Hogwarts—the Forbidden Forest. Second, he comes face to face with a hooded figure drinking the unicorn's blood, and his scar erupts in pain. Third, and most importantly, Harry realizes the hooded figure was actually Voldemort and guesses that Snape is after the Sorcerer's Stone to help Voldemort come back to power. When writing a pivotal scene in your own novel, consider how you can play with the stakes of your global genre in multiple ways to achieve the most impact. In this scene in particular, the hooded figure (Quirrell/Voldemort) "attacks" Harry more directly than ever before when he approaches him in the Forbidden Forest. Although there's no direct physical altercation, Harry's scar erupts in pain, and Harry falls to the ground. Because this is a middle-grade novel, this is an age-appropriate escalation of the global stakes.
- This scene includes a great example of an implied crisis, or a crisis that isn't one hundred percent on the page. Harry is literally frozen in fear and pain, unable to move, let alone save himself. This kind of crisis does two important things. First, it reminds us of Harry's age and skillset because, in this book, he's an eleven-year-old first-year wizard with very little experience. By the end of the series, we will be able to gauge how much Harry's grown and changed based on how he responds in moments like these compared to the first book. Second, this shows us the power divide between Harry and Voldemort. Even though Voldemort is not at his full power, he's still able to have a significant effect on Harry. As readers, this will enable us to feel properly worried for Harry in the global Climax.
- Notice that Firenze is different from the other centaurs because he cares about saving lives, whether centaur or human. This is important for two reasons. First, this establishes Firenze as a

character that Harry (and readers) can trust. And second, this is a wonderful echo of the story's theme. Firenze, like Harry, is willing to sacrifice for others without letting prejudice get in the way. Conversely, Bane and the other centaurs are behaving more like Voldemort here, only concerned with their own agenda. As writers, we can use side characters like this to give our themes more depth and emotional impact.

SCENE 23
THROUGH THE TRAPDOOR
CHAPTER 16

2,389 words

"In years to come, Harry would ... throwing me out after that"

Summary: Hagrid confirms he *did* tell the stranger at the Hog's Head how to get past Fluffy, and Harry is horrified at this news. They try to find Dumbledore but run into McGonagall who tells them Dumbledore has gone to London. Harry realizes the stone is vulnerable while Dumbledore's away, so they decide to do what they can to protect it in Dumbledore's absence, but all of their plans fail. Because of this, Harry decides to go after the stone himself. Harry concludes if he doesn't die tonight, Voldemort will return to power and kill him eventually.

ANALYZING THE SCENE

STORY EVENT

A Story Event is an active change of a universal human value for one or more characters as a result of conflict (one character's desires clash with

another's, or an environmental shift changes the value positively or negatively).

A Working Scene contains at least one Story Event. To determine a scene's Story Event, answer these four Socratic questions:

1. What are the characters literally doing—that is, what are their micro on-the-surface actions? Reader's Perspective (OTS)

Harry talks to Hagrid about the stranger who gave him the dragon egg and to McGonagall about Dumbledore. After that, Harry, Ron, and Hermione try to keep an eye on Snape in Dumbledore's absence but fail and get sent back to their dormitory.

OTS Change (Harry): Hogwarts Castle to Hagrid's Hut to the Entrance Hall

2. What is the essential tactic of the characters—that is, what above-the-surface macro behaviors are they employing that are linked to a universal human value? Character's Perspective (ATS)

Harry, Ron, and Hermione want to find out if Hagrid told a stranger about how to get past Fluffy because if he did, that would leave Snape open to steal the stone. After confirming this from Hagrid, the three friends want to tell Dumbledore what they know, but McGonagall dismisses the severity of the situation and tells them not to worry, even though Dumbledore is gone. Their focus then shifts to protecting the stone while Dumbledore's gone, but their plan fails so they decide to go after the stone themselves.

ATS Change (Harry): Relying on Adults to Relying on Self

3. What beyond-the-surface universal human values have changed for one or more characters in the scene? Which one of those value changes is most important and should be included in the Story Grid Spreadsheet? Author's Perspective (BTS)

Harry is left unprotected without Dumbledore's presence in the castle. Because of this, he can no longer be passive, hoping Dumbledore will stop

Snape. He has to take matters into his own hands since other adults, specifically McGonagall, don't seem worried. Harry believes the stone is going to be stolen tonight, which it will be if he doesn't stop Quirrell (even though Harry thinks he needs to stop Snape). To put his life on the line to stop "Snape" is to risk death, but to not do anything guarantees death if Voldemort returns to power.

BTS Change (Harry): *Protected to Unprotected*

4. The Scene Event Synthesis: What Story Event sums up the scene's on-the-surface, above-the-surface, and beyond-the-surface change? We will enter that event in the Story Grid Spreadsheet.

After learning Dumbledore has left the castle, Harry, Ron, and Hermione decide to go after the stone so they can get it before Snape does and keep it safe.

HOW THE SCENE ABIDES BY THE FIVE COMMANDMENTS OF STORYTELLING

Inciting Incident: Causal. Hagrid confirms that he might have accidentally told the stranger in the Hog's Head how to get past Fluffy.

Turning Point Progressive Complication: Revelatory. Harry, Ron, and Hermione learn that Dumbledore has left the castle, and they're convinced Snape will go after the stone tonight.

Crisis: Best Bad Choice. Should Harry risk expulsion (or death) to prevent Snape from acquiring the stone for Voldemort? Or should he trust the adults to protect the stone and stay out of the conflict but risk Snape succeeding and Voldemort coming back to full power, killing him eventually anyway?

Climax: Harry decides he will go after the stone tonight.

Resolution: Hermione and Ron agree to help Harry despite the risks.

NOTES

- This is the global Crisis of the story and the Inciting Incident of the Ending Payoff. Harry clearly states what's at stake should he not act. He says, "If I get caught before I can get to the stone, well, I'll have to go back to the Dursleys and wait for Voldemort to find me there, it's only dying a bit later than I would have, because I'm never going over to the Dark Side!" This is definitely a best bad choice for Harry!
- Although this scene spans multiple locations and includes multiple different character interactions, I analyzed it as one scene because everything contributes to one primary development: Harry learns the Sorcerer's Stone is at risk *tonight* and decides to go after it himself. When they realize Hagrid told the stranger how to get past Fluffy, they seek out Dumbledore. When they learn Dumbledore has left the castle, they decide to try and guard the stone themselves. And finally, when that plan fails, they decide to go after the stone themselves in the next scene. Each of these smaller moments acts as a Progressive Complication, and the overarching scene forces Harry, Ron, and Hermione to *choose* to go after the stone versus relying on the adults to protect it.
- The external Action genre shifts negatively in this scene. Harry and his friends were relatively safe, but now they're headed toward danger—especially because Dumbledore is gone. That being said, the internal Worldview genre shifts positively, though it doesn't feel like it for Harry in the moment. Harry's finally taking control of his own destiny!
- Dumbledore's gone because he received an urgent owl from the Ministry of Magic. Harry thinks Snape sent the note, but it was actually Professor Quirrell. Although McGonagall tells Harry, Ron, and Hermione to drop it, Harry can't help but follow his instinct and act on what he thinks he knows. This common theme pops up again and again in the Harry Potter series.

Should Harry listen to himself, or should he listen to the adults? More often than not, Harry chooses to listen to himself even if it means breaking the rules.
- This scene pays off all the clues laid about Hagrid and his love for dragons. We now know how Hagrid got the dragon egg and that he was just a pawn in Voldemort's scheme. Poor Hagrid!

SCENE 24

THROUGH THE TRAPDOOR

CHAPTER 16

4,010 words

"After dinner, the three of ... side, in the last chamber."

Summary: Later that night, Harry, Ron, and Hermione go through the trapdoor on the third floor and navigate the various obstacles waiting for them—Devil's Snare, flying keys, an enchanted chess board, an unconscious mountain troll, and a potion-puzzle to solve. Ron sacrifices himself during the chess game so Hermione and Harry can continue on, but when they realize there's only enough potion to let one of them through the final chamber, Harry decides to go on alone.

ANALYZING THE SCENE

STORY EVENT

A Story Event is an active change of a universal human value for one or more characters as a result of conflict (one character's desires clash with

another's, or an environmental shift changes the value positively or negatively).

A Working Scene contains at least one Story Event. To determine a scene's Story Event, answer these four Socratic questions:

1. **What are the characters literally doing—that is, what are their micro on-the-surface actions? Reader's Perspective (OTS)**

Harry, Ron, and Hermione sneak out of the dormitory, go through the trapdoor, and face multiple obstacles to prevent Snape from bringing the stone to Voldemort.

OTS Change (Harry): Gryffindor Common Room to Under the School

2. **What is the essential tactic of the characters—that is, what above-the-surface macro behaviors are they employing that are linked to a universal human value? Character's Perspective (ATS)**

Quirrell wants to take advantage of Dumbledore's absence to retrieve the Sorcerer's Stone for Voldemort, but Harry, Ron, and Hermione want to prevent that from happening, even though they still suspect Snape. Several enchanted obstacles want to prevent the kids from reaching the stone because they have been created to do so.

ATS Change (Harry): Together to Separate / Stopping Snape to Acquiring the Stone

3. **What beyond-the-surface universal human values have changed for one or more characters in the scene? Which one of those value changes is most important and should be included in the Story Grid Spreadsheet? Author's Perspective (BTS)**

Harry and his friends face multiple levels of danger as they race to the innermost chamber beneath the trapdoor. In the face of each obstacle, it becomes increasingly more apparent why Harry's choice in friends impacts his ability to survive. However, in the end, Harry must be the one to face Voldemort. This means that while Harry's courage and humility—two of his special gifts—show positive change in his Worldview story arc, he's coming closer and closer to meeting Voldemort face to face and risking death.

BTS Change (Harry): *Unprotected to Imminent Danger*

4. **The Scene Event Synthesis: What Story Event sums up the scene's on-the-surface, above-the-surface, and beyond-the-surface change? We will enter that event in the Story Grid Spreadsheet.**

Harry faces various levels of danger once he and his friends navigate the obstacles underneath the school.

HOW THE SCENE ABIDES BY THE FIVE COMMANDMENTS OF STORYTELLING

Inciting Incident: Causal. The trapdoor is open, which means Snape's already gotten past Fluffy.

Turning Point Progressive Complication: Active. There's only enough potion for either Harry or Hermione to go through to the final chamber, and he's already lost Ron.

Crisis: Best Bad Choice. Should Harry continue on alone and risk coming face to face with Snape (Quirrell/Voldemort) alone? Or should he go back and allow Snape (Quirrell/Voldemort) to acquire the Sorcerer's Stone?

Climax: Harry drinks the potion; he will go forward alone.

Resolution: Hermione heads back to the castle and Harry enters the final chamber alone.

NOTES

- This is the Turning Point and Crisis of the Ending Payoff. Harry's scene goal is to get to the stone before Snape can. Once he sees the trapdoor is already open, his goal shifts slightly. Now, he wants to stop Snape from getting *and using* the stone, assuming Snape's already beaten him to it. Each obstacle they face along the way acts as a Progressive Complication for the overarching scene—including Harry losing his friends one by one. First, he loses Ron, and then he loses Hermione and must decide between going through to the final chamber alone or heading back to the castle and letting Voldemort win.
- Although Harry decides to go on alone, he asks Hermione to send word to Dumbledore. This gives us the sense that Harry still doubts his own abilities (rightly so since he's a first-year) and still expects the adults to solve his problems. So, although he's moved closer to competence, he still has some learning and coming into his own to do.
- This scene provides a great example of the difference between Harry and Voldemort—something that will determine the death or survival of each. Harry trusts and relies on his friends while Voldemort uses and manipulates his followers. Harry refuses to turn Dark despite the risk of death. This humility is Harry's special gift, even if acting on it brings him closer to physical death on the Action value spectrum.
- Neville has an arc of change in this story, too. Here, we see him finally reach his breaking point. He does not want Harry, Ron, Hermione (and Gryffindor) to get into any more trouble. The best part is that he's later rewarded by Dumbledore for standing up to his friends!
- Did you notice that each obstacle corresponds with a different Hogwarts teacher? Not only that, but they all require skills that Harry, Ron, and Hermione have learned throughout the year. The situation allows us to see Harry, Ron, and Hermione use skills that are unique to each of them, too. For example, Ron takes charge of the chess game, Harry uses his flying skills, and

Hermione relies on her logic. Not only do we see a change in each of their confidence levels, but we see a change in their competence in magic as well. Also, the tasks get harder and harder to pass through, too. Harry can recover the flying key on his own. We know he's a skilled flier, but he needs Ron to help him past wizard's chess and Hermione to help him pass the potions riddle. We're seeing their "gifts expressed," which makes for a satisfying reading experience!

SCENE 25

THE MAN WITH TWO FACES

CHAPTER 17

1,882 words

"There was already someone there ... into blackness, down ... down ... down ..."

Summary: Quirrell admits he's been behind everything that's happened to Harry this year and confirms he's after the Sorcerer's Stone. Quirrell demands Harry look into the mirror, hoping he'll see the location of the Sorcerer's Stone, but to Harry's surprise he feels the stone drop into his pocket instead. When Harry lies to Quirrell about what he sees in the mirror, Quirrell unwraps his turban, revealing Voldemort, and Voldemort tells Harry it's better to join him and hand over the stone than be killed. Harry declines Voldemort's offer, they face off, and his scar erupts in pain, causing him to lose consciousness.

ANALYZING THE SCENE

STORY EVENT

A Story Event is an active change of a universal human value for one or more characters as a result of conflict (one character's desires clash with another's, or an environmental shift changes the value positively or negatively).

A Working Scene contains at least one Story Event. To determine a scene's Story Event, answer these four Socratic questions:

1. What are the characters literally doing—that is, what are their micro on-the-surface actions? Reader's Perspective (OTS)

Harry talks to Quirrell in front of the Mirror of Erised and faces off with Voldemort.
OTS Change (Harry): In Danger to Unconscious / Final Chamber to Unknown

2. What is the essential tactic of the characters—that is, what above-the-surface macro behaviors are they employing that are linked to a universal human value? Character's Perspective (ATS)

Voldemort wants the Sorcerer's Stone so he can come back to life/power, but Harry wants to prevent him from acquiring and using it.
ATS Change (Harry): Sacrificial to Heroic

3. What beyond-the-surface universal human values have changed for one or more characters in the scene? Which one of those value changes is most important and should be included in the Story Grid Spreadsheet? Author's Perspective (BTS)

Although Voldemort is a very powerful dark wizard, he and Harry are evenly matched because Voldemort cannot operate with his full power. That being said, Quirrell *is* a very dangerous and powerful wizard who *can* use his full power, which means Harry is in immediate physical danger and could potentially lose his life in this scene, despite Voldemort's current physical condition. However, because of Harry's humility and selflessness, he's able to prevent Voldemort and Quirrell from acquiring the stone. Although Harry ends the scene unconscious, his actions are proof of Harry's maturity and willingness to embrace his destiny as The Boy Who Lived.

BTS Change (Harry): *Danger to Unconscious*

4. The Scene Event Synthesis: What Story Event sums up the scene's on-the-surface, above-the-surface, and beyond-the-surface change? We will enter that event in the Story Grid Spreadsheet.

Harry faces and defeats Quirrell and Voldemort and saves the Sorcerer's Stone.

HOW THE SCENE ABIDES BY THE FIVE COMMANDMENTS OF STORYTELLING

Inciting Incident: Causal. Quirrell is in the chamber, not Snape.

Turning Point Progressive Complication: Active. Voldemort demands that Harry give him the Sorcerer's Stone that's in his pocket.

Crisis: Best Bad Choice. Should he give Voldemort the stone to avoid meeting the same end as his parents? Or should he keep the stone and risk being killed anyway?

Climax: Harry does not give up the stone.

Resolution: Quirrell attacks Harry, but touching Harry causes him to blister. Harry presses his hands on Quirrell's face and then blacks out.

NOTES

- This is the global Climax and the Climax of the Ending Payoff. Notice how Rowling handled the power divide in this scene. If Voldemort was at his full power, there's no way Harry would be able to best him in this scene. However, Rowling found a creative solution to this problem. She leveled the playing field by stripping Voldemort of his body and power, making him and Harry more evenly matched. As readers, we still worry about Harry's ability to defeat Voldemort, and it's crystal clear that his life is at stake in this scene, especially because of Quirrell's presence and actions. However, it makes sense, and we buy into it because of the way Rowling set up the story and this scene. Here, the stakes are at their highest and Quirrell/Voldemort directly attacks Harry to the point of rendering him unconscious. Again, because this is a middle-grade novel, this is a great example of an age-appropriate Climax that meets the Action genre requirements.
- This scene also includes a great example of how writers can craft their protagonist and their antagonist to be opposite sides of the same coin. Voldemort uses and manipulates others for his own end, but Harry is willing to sacrifice himself so others can survive. Harry's selflessness and his willingness to sacrifice, along with his mother's love and protection, of course, help him defeat Voldemort in this climactic moment.

SCENE 26

THE MAN WITH TWO FACES

CHAPTER 17

3,570 words

"Something gold was glinting just ...fun with Dudley this summer..."

Summary: Harry wakes up in the hospital wing to Dumbledore hovering at his bedside. Dumbledore explains how Harry saved the Sorcerer's Stone and says that it's since been destroyed. Harry asks about Voldemort, and Dumbledore confirms that he's still out there somewhere, likely waiting for the next opportunity to come back to power. Harry asks Dumbledore why Voldemort tried to kill him in the first place, but Dumbledore refuses to answer. They talk some more about Harry's parents and how Harry got the stone out of the mirror, but eventually Dumbledore leaves. Later, Hagrid visits and then Ron and Hermione. At the end-of-year feast, Dumbledore awards Harry, Ron, Hermione, and Neville points for their courage and bravery, putting Gryffindor back in first place and allowing them to win the House Cup. The school year comes to a close, and Harry heads back to the Dursleys' for summer break.

ANALYZING THE SCENE

STORY EVENT

A Story Event is an active change of a universal human value for one or more characters as a result of conflict (one character's desires clash with another's, or an environmental shift changes the value positively or negatively).

A Working Scene contains at least one Story Event. To determine a scene's Story Event, answer these four Socratic questions:

1. **What are the characters literally doing—that is, what are their micro on-the-surface actions? Reader's Perspective (OTS)**

Harry wakes up in the hospital wing and talks to Dumbledore, Hagrid, Ron, and Hermione.
OTS Change (Harry): Unconscious to Conscious

2. **What is the essential tactic of the characters—that is, what above-the-surface macro behaviors are they employing that are linked to a universal human value? Character's Perspective (ATS)**

Harry wants answers about what happened in the final chamber with Voldemort, and he wants to know more about his past, too. However, Dumbledore wants to keep some things a secret from Harry (for reasons unknown in this book), so he tells him only as much of the truth as he feels comfortable sharing.
ATS Change (Harry): Ignorance to Knowledge

3. **What beyond-the-surface universal human values have changed for one or more characters in the scene? Which one of those value changes is most important and should be included in the Story Grid Spreadsheet? Author's Perspective- BTS**

Harry has temporarily defeated Voldemort and is safely recovering in the hospital wing. However, Dumbledore makes it clear that Voldemort is still out there somewhere, waiting for his next opportunity to return to power.

BTS Change (Harry): *Ignorance to Knowledge*

4. The Scene Event Synthesis: What Story Event sums up the scene's on-the-surface, above-the-surface, and beyond-the-surface change? We will enter that event in the Story Grid Spreadsheet.

Harry recovers from his injuries in the hospital wing and learns about Voldemort (and himself) from Dumbledore.

HOW THE SCENE ABIDES BY THE FIVE COMMANDMENTS OF STORYTELLING

Inciting Incident: Causal. Harry wakes up in the hospital wing with Dumbledore by his bedside.

Turning Point Progressive Complication: Active. Dumbledore refuses to answer Harry's question about why Voldemort tried to kill him when he was a baby.

Crisis: Best Bad Choice. Should Harry push for more information? Or should he trust that Dumbledore has his best interest and not argue?

Climax: Harry does not argue.

Resolution: Harry's rewarded with *different* information. Dumbledore answers all of Harry's other questions about what happened in the final chamber and about Snape's relationship with Harry's father. After that Ron and Hermione visit, Hagrid visits, the students attend the end-of-year banquet (where Gryffindor is awarded the House Cup), and finally they all head home for the summer.

NOTES

- This scene contains the Resolution of the Ending Payoff *and* the Resolution of the global story. It's a satisfying scene because we get a lot of questions answered. Plus, each moment within the scene (Harry talking to Dumbledore, Harry talking to Ron and Hermione, Harry talking to Hagrid, the end-of-year banquet, and Harry returning to Privet Drive) hits the same emotional note—Harry is safe from Voldemort, and he's found a place to belong at Hogwarts. He's also *proven* to himself that he *is* The Boy Who Lived.
- Notice the way Rowling delivers information through a conversation between Harry and Dumbledore. This works because Harry is truly naive to the answers. If Harry grew up in the wizarding world, or if he was fully conscious during the previous scene, a conversation like this wouldn't work.
- This is a satisfying moment because Dumbledore confirms what we just saw in the last scene, too. Harry's selflessness and his mother's love ultimately helped him defeat Voldemort. This is a great way to hit home the theme or lesson of the story for readers by first showing it in the previous scene, and then confirming it through a later conversation.
- This line of dialogue sums up every Harry Potter book, "I think he sort of wanted to give me a chance. I think he knows more or less everything that goes on here, you know. I reckon he had a pretty good idea we were going to try, and instead of stopping us, he just taught us enough to help." It's clear that Dumbledore has faith in Harry and trusts him to handle big things. This creates a safe and nurturing space for Harry to build his character and ultimately develop into the Chosen One who will defeat Voldemort in the end.

FINAL THOUGHTS

Hopefully, you can see why we consider *Harry Potter and the Sorcerer's Stone* to be a true Action story Masterwork. Rowling not only met readers' expectations but exceeded them in big ways. And by doing so, she created a story that will stick with readers until the end of time. If you want to write a book like this, here ten key takeaways we learned when putting together this masterwork guide:

1. It fits within the Action/Worldview genre framework.
The external plot and the internal character are woven together so expertly that Harry cannot succeed in his mission to stop Voldemort from acquiring the Sorcerer's Stone without overcoming his inner obstacle. When writing your own Action/Worldview story, consider how the external and internal key scenes and conventions weave together to create an impactful and immersive experience for readers.

2. The stakes are appropriate for middle-grade readers.
Although this is an Action story with life-or-death stakes, Harry's life is really only at stake in the global climax when he faces Quirrell/Voldemort alone. That being said, Rowling does an excellent job growing, escalating, and complicating the stakes from the start of the book all the way to the end. When writing your own middle-grade book (or Action story), brain-

storm unique ways to deliver on the genre requirements (in terms of what's at stake) while always keeping in mind the age range of your target audience.

3. Harry is an underdog protagonist that you can't help but root for from the start.

Although most middle-grade readers will never get the chance to go to a school for witches and wizards (darn it!) or have to go face to face with the most powerful Dark Lord to survive (thank goodness), we all know what it's like to have moments of self-doubt, longing, and fear. When crafting your own story, consider how you can play on universal themes like love, friendship, and belonging to pull the reader in and get them to root for your protagonist. Plus, don't discount the cast of truly compelling (and quirky) characters Rowling created! When crafting your own cast of characters, you can take inspiration from how she created a cast with varied backgrounds, ages, professions, emotions, and viewpoints—all of whom help readers of all ages and cultures relate.

4. This story has heart.

It plays on universal themes like love, friendship, belonging, and having courage in the face of uncertainty. The external plot events wouldn't be as exciting or memorable if such a strong internal arc wasn't running alongside it. When crafting your own story, make sure you're crystal clear on your theme (a.k.a. the message you want to share with readers) and consider all the different ways the external conflict in your plot can put pressure on your character's internal obstacle, forcing them to grow and change.

5. The story world evokes feelings of wonder, which is a must for any fantasy story!

That being said, notice how Rowling focused her world-building efforts on a few key areas in this first book. There's *a lot* we don't learn about until later in the series, and that's okay! When creating the world for your own fantasy story, always consider the reader's experience and give them just enough to understand what's happening in any given scene but not enough to weigh them down in a bunch of unnecessary information. And make sure to consider the age range of your target audience, too. Readers of all ages want to experience a story world that evokes wonder, but middle-grade readers require more of a learning curve than older audiences do.

6. Multiple forces of antagonism are at work.
This gives Rowling room to create red herrings and provide conflict for Harry on a day-to-day basis when Voldemort/Quirrell is not present or able to do so. Without characters like Draco Malfoy and Professor Snape, there wouldn't be enough conflict to keep the story moving forward. If you want to write an antagonist that's off the page for most of the book (like Voldemort is), make sure you have enough day-to-day conflict for your protagonist to face to keep the story interesting and to force them to grow and change. And don't forget to play up the similarities and differences between your protagonist and antagonist, too! This will help you explore all the different sides of your central conflict and theme.

7. Each scene moves multiple plotlines (and character arcs) forward.
Rowling is a master at layering storylines together within a scene. There's not a lot of "fluff" in this book! When writing a middle-grade story, you don't have a lot of room word-count-wise (most middle-grade books are about twenty thousand to fifty thousand words, with more allowance given to fantasy novels that require world-building), so you have to make every scene count. Throughout the analysis, you may have noticed that I did not determine scene breaks by a change in setting or a change in the cast of characters but rather by a change in Value. This Value impacts the global story, and it also shifts when the goal in the scene is either accomplished or lost. Even if you're not following the time/space/distance rule of "a scene," you can still manage to write a compelling scene as long as the goal and value shift are clear and strong. This supersedes time, space, and distance because we're so focused on the character succeeding that we'll go anywhere with them, even if the setting or cast of characters changes.

8. Questions are raised (and answered) throughout the story.
This keeps the reader forever looking forward, turning page after page to find out what happens next. When writing your own stories, consider what you want readers to be curious about at the end of each scene and make

sure enough questions are raised (and answered) throughout the book to hold their interest.

9. The point of view is (mostly) consistent.
We experience the story from Harry's perspective except for a few times when Rowling dips into other characters' heads. Keeping the point of view consistent and making intentional decisions about point of view allow the reader to sink into the story and become fully immersed. When writing your own stories, don't discount the power of point of view. Make a deliberate choice and use it to your advantage!

10. There's humor, which middle-grade readers love!
From throwing snowballs at Professor Quirrell's turban to Hagrid hoping his dragon will call him "mummy," there's plenty of humor and silliness in this book. If you're writing for a middle-grade audience, consider how you can play with humor in your own story because it's super important!

So, there you have it! I hope this analysis has helped you see all the moving parts that go into writing a story like *Harry Potter and the Sorcerer's Stone*, and I hope that in seeing those moving parts, the bigger task of writing a novel has become less overwhelming. If I could leave you with one final piece of advice, it's this: Always remember that the purpose of your first draft is to discover what your story's really about. It's not to write something that's perfect. Once you get the story down on paper, you can use the tools presented in this masterwork guide to analyze your draft and make the next version of your story even better!

Mischief Managed!

AUTHOR'S NOTE

If you enjoyed reading this book, would you mind leaving an honest review? Your reviews help other people find this book and decide whether they want to read it. Plus, they're really fun for us to read, too. We love hearing your feedback!

https://mybook.to/hpssmasterwork

NOTES

- The 2018 MarketWatch article about *Harry Potter and the Sorcerer's Stone* spending 481 weeks on the *USA Today's* Best-Selling Books list https://www.marketwatch.com/story/the-25-billion-wizarding-world-of-harry-potter-by-the-numbers-2018-08-30
- The 2021 WordsRated article with sales stats and facts on the Harry Potter series https://wordsrated.com/harry-potter-stats/
- The 2021WordsRated article that includes sales stats and facts on the Harry Potter series https://wordsrated.com/harry-potter-stats/
- The 2005 interview with MuggleNet and the Leaky Cauldron where Rowling talks about what Voldemort would see in the Mirror of Erised http://www.accio-quote.org/articles/2005/0705-tlc_mugglenet-anelli-2.htm
- Action Story: The Primal Genre by Shawn Coyne https://store.storygrid.com/product/action-story/
- In addition to the Story Grid Spreadsheet for *Harry Potter and the Sorcerer's Stone*, you can view the Story Grid Foolscap and the actual Story Grid Infographic at https://www.storygrid.com/masterwork/Harry-Potter-and-the-Sorcerers-Stone

ABOUT THE AUTHOR

SAVANNAH GILBO is a proud Ravenclaw, developmental editor, and book coach who helps fiction authors write, edit, and publish stories that work. She's also the host of the top-rated Fiction Writing Made Easy Podcast, where she delivers weekly episodes full of simple, actionable, and step-by-step strategies that you can implement in your writing right away. When she's not busy crafting her own stories, you can find Savannah curled up with a good book, a cozy blanket, and her three perfect puppies.

CONNECT WITH SAVANNAH:

Website: www.savannahgilbo.com
Instagram: @savannah.gilbo
Podcast: Fiction Writing Made Easy

ABOUT THE EDITOR

ABIGAIL K. PERRY is a proud Gryffindor, developmental editor, and book coach who specializes in Upmarket (Book Club) Fiction, Women's Fiction, Curio Fiction, and YA Fantasy. She has studied storytelling for over a decade and holds a B.S. in TV, Radio, and Film from Syracuse University (Newhouse) and a Masters in Secondary Education, English from Endicott College. Abigail taught creative writing and film for a handful of years and has held several internships in publishing and film, including one as an editorial intern at P.S. Literary Agency (where she later worked as the Agency Relations Assistant).

Eager to support writers on their path to publishing, Abigail created the Lit Match podcast, where she teaches writers how to blend passion with business so they can hook their ideal literary agent and build fruitful careers. Abigail is also the author of the Story Grid Masterwork Guide featuring *Hamilton*.

Abigail currently lives in Massachusetts with her husband, two children, and rescue pup. She is constantly looking for stories with big emotions and adventures and any and every opportunity to quote a book or movie, spend time with loved ones and animals, travel, go for a long walk, and, in general, explore outside.

CONNECT WITH ABIGAIL:

Website: www.abigailkperry.com
Instagram: @abigailkperry
Podcast: Lit Match

Made in the USA
Coppell, TX
01 August 2024

35425949R00115